domain.456

The Invisible World
My Values
Sin

Kersten Hamilton, Ellen Larson, and Linda Kondracki-Sibley

David C Cook®

transforming lives together

domain.456: The Invisible World, My Values, Sin
© 1991, 2003 by David C. Cook
Published by David C. Cook
4050 Lee Vance View
Colorado Springs, CO 80918 U.S.A.

David C. Cook Distribution Canada
55 Woodslee Avenue, Paris, Ontario, Canada N3L 3E5

David C. Cook U.K., Kingsway Communications
Eastbourne, East Sussex BN23 6NT, England

David C. Cook and the graphic circle C logo are registered trademarks of Cook Communications
Ministries.

All rights reserved. Except for the reproducible Activity Sheets, which may be copied for classroom
use, and the newsletter *PARTNERS*, which may be copied for distribution to parents, no part of this
book may be reproduced or used in any form without the written permission of the publisher, unless
otherwise noted in the text.

Scripture quotations are taken from the HOLY BIBLE, NEW INTERNATIONAL VERSION®. Copyright
© 1973, 1978, 1984 by International Bible Society. Used by permission of Zondervan. All rights
reserved.

Cover Design: Sonya Duckworth
Interior Design: Jeff Jansen
Additional Interior Design: Sonya Duckworth, Erica Whitcombe
Illustrations: Sonny Carder
Editor: Rick Wesselhoff

ISBN 978-0-7814-5462-9

Printed in the United States
First Printing 1991

6 7 8 9 10 11 12 13 14 15

Table of Contents

Welcome to the domain.456 Series

✔ Let's Talk about It

What is it like to grow up in North America today? Every day your students are confronted with a number of issues previous generations didn't have to deal with. Classmates wielding knives and guns. Some of them injured or even killed in gang-related incidents. And dire reports about everything from AIDS to ecological concerns warning them their planet may not exist by the time they "grow up." What's more, larger and larger numbers of upper elementary-age students are experiencing problems closer to home, from divorce to sexual abuse to the struggles of growing up with just one parent.

What can we do to help? Today's world can be a scary place for preteens. As adults, we have two choices: We can spend our time longing for the way it used to be, or we can realize that today's students need a place where they can talk about these issues. Instead of wishing for simpler days, its time for us to say to our children, "Let's talk about it . . . ."

This series was designed to help you do just that. Each unit in this series is based on an issue upper elementary-age children are concerned about. In many cases your students are already learning about these issues from their peers, their schools, and the media. With this curriculum, you can provide them with the opportunity to discuss their concerns in a distinctly Christian context.

✔ Features of the domain.456 Series

Flexibility and Variety

The domain.456 series can be used effectively in any number of settings, including:
- Sunday school
- Midweek meetings
- Retreats, or other special events

Four-Part Lesson Plan

Each lesson follows this format:

1. Setting the Stage (5-10 minutes)—Each lesson begins with an activity designed to do two things. First, it is designed to be a *gathering activity*, which means you can involve your students in it as they arrive instead of waiting until everyone gets there. Second, the Setting the Stage activity is designed to *grab children's attention*. In a fun and interesting way, it will whet your students' appetite to hear about an issue that's important to them.

Teacher Tip: Arrive early and have the activity ready to go before the first student arrives. This will help you communicate a sense of excitement about the lesson and set a tone of orderliness for your class.

2. Introducing the Issue (20 minutes)—This section of the lesson will involve the students in an active discussion of the lesson's topic. Each Introducing the Issue activity contains information students need to know about the topic, ideas for one or more learning activities that will help you present that information, and follow-up questions that will get students talking about important issues.

Teacher Tip: As you lead your students into the lesson, establish your class as a place where everyone's feelings and questions are welcomed (some suggestions for doing that are listed on page 5). You just might be amazed at the depth of your students' thinking and the quality of your discussions.

3. Searching the Scriptures (20 minutes)—This section of the lesson takes your class straight to the Bible. Through a wide variety of creative teaching methods, your students will study people and principles of Scripture that speak directly to the contemporary issue being discussed. For some of your students, this may be the first time they hear that God has the answers about the issues that matter to them.

Teacher Tip: Whenever possible, don't just lecture about what the Bible says, teach students how to use the Bible themselves. You will be equipping them with the most valuable resource they have for coping with contemporary issues: God's Word.

4. Living the Lesson (5-10 minutes)—Each lesson ends by challenging your students to take what they've learned and apply it to their own lives. Living the Lesson will encourage each student to ask, "What am I going to do with what I've just learned?"

Teacher Tip: One of the best ways to help students apply biblical truth to their lives is to share with them how you have learned to apply the Scriptures. Look for opportunities to share with your students the ways that you have applied God's Word to your life.

Clearly Stated Key Principles

Each book contains three units, and each unit addresses a different topic of concern. The following four features will help your students focus on and remember the central principles of each unit.

1. The Unit Verse summarizes the biblical principle central to the unit topic. The meaning of the verse is developed a little more each week as students work through activities designed to help them understand and apply a key biblical principle.

2. The Unit Affirmation is the primary learning objective of the unit. Each Unit Affirmation begins with "I CAN. . . ." Students hear many negative messages. All too often, they hear what they *can't* do. The Unit Affirmation helps them focus on something positive they *can* do. Students spend time each week repeating the Unit Affirmation and discussing how it applies to what they've learned.

3. The Unit Poster reinforces the Unit Verse and Unit Affirmation. At the beginning of each unit you will find a Unit Poster page that includes the Unit Verse, Unit Affirmation, and artwork. Photocopy the Unit Poster page onto a transparency and put the transparency on an overhead projector. Trace the enlarged image onto a piece of posterboard or newsprint. You might recruit students to help you trace and color the poster. Each lesson contains a suggestion for how to use the Unit Poster.

4. Unit Service Projects are optional activities you can do with students outside of class. You can find a list of service projects at the end of each unit. Taking the time to involve your class in at least one unit project will help the students see that they can take an active role in the issues that affect their lives.

Parent Newsletter

Each unit includes a new issue of *PARTNERS*, a newsletter you can photocopy and send home to the parents (or guardians) of each class member. This letter gives parents an overview of the topic being studied. It also gives ideas for families to practice together the biblical principles learned in each unit.

✓ A Word about Children and Stress . . .

As you prepare to teach the domain.456 series, it is important to realize that many of the issues covered in this series can be sources of stress for your students. Many students have never had the chance to talk openly about these kinds of issues, and doing so in your class may well raise their anxiety level. There are several things you can keep in mind to help students feel more comfortable:

1) Point them to Jesus. While today's children may be growing up faster than we like, the good news is there is nothing too tough for them to handle with Jesus' help. By leading them through the Bible studies and talking about the power of Christ in your own life, you can point students to Jesus. You will have the privilege of introducing some students to Jesus for the first time. You will also have the opportunity to help Christian students deepen their faith. By helping children learn to walk through life with Jesus, you will give them the one thing that can best help them cope with life.

2) Create a safe place where they can talk about their real feelings. Children have a tendency to say the things in class they think teachers want to hear. You will want to continually reassure your children that they can say what is really on their minds. Early in this series you should establish ground rules for your discussions. Most important among those rules: No one can criticize or make fun of anything anyone else shares in class. Once children know that whatever they say will be accepted by you and the rest of the class, they will feel much safer.

3) If necessary, refer students to outside help. You may find a child in your class who is experiencing an unusual amount of stress. In that case, ask your pastor or Christian Education Director for the procedure your church uses to refer children and families for professional help.

Shedding Light on the Invisible World

Your students are at the age where they are just beginning to think in abstract terms. As a result, they are starting to ask important questions about the spiritual world—a world that is invisible, yet very powerful and relevant to their lives. In addition, everywhere students look they are bombarded with television shows, movies, and books about psychic powers, alien abductions, and counterfeit religions. How can they find out what's true and what's counterfeit when it comes to the invisible world?

Over the next five weeks, you will have the opportunity to explore the invisible world with your students. You will test modern myths and ideologies against the Bible, our truth source about the invisible world. God is the author and creator of the unseen world. By focusing on His truth and His Word, we can teach our students to identify spiritual counterfeits!

Invisible World Overview

Unit Verse: Your word is truth. John 17:17b
Unit Affirmation: I CAN USE THE BIBLE TO JUDGE WHAT'S TRUE ABOUT THE INVISIBLE WORLD!

LESSON	TITLE	AIM	SCRIPTURE BASE
Lesson #1	The Truth Is in There	Students will understand they can find the truth about the invisible world in the Bible.	Matthew 4:1-11
Lesson #2	For Heaven's Sake!	Students will understand what the Bible says about heaven and learn to identify "counterfeit" ideas about the afterlife.	John 14:2-3; 1 Corinthians 15:42-44; Revelation 21:1-4; 22:1-4
Lesson #3	Touched by Angels	Students will understand what the Bible says about angels and learn to identify "counterfeit" ideas about angels.	Hebrews 1:14; Psalm 91:9-12; and other passages
Lesson #4	Junk Power	Students will understand what the Bible says about God's supernatural powers and learn to identify "counterfeit" supernatural powers that don't honor God.	1 Samuel 28:12-18; Deuteronomy 18:9-13
Lesson #5	The Final Chapter	Students will understand that God is in control of the future and has already won the war with Satan.	Matthew 24:3-14; 36-42; Acts 2:17-21; Revelation 19:11-24; Titus 2:11-14
Also, see page 48 for a list of optional service projects for this unit.			

Partners

Students Explore the Invisible World!

DEAR PARENTS: We hope this newsletter helps keep you informed about and involved in what we're doing. After all, you are your children's most important spiritual leaders. We want to be your partner any way we can.

Have you ever been fooled by someone trying to pass off a purple piece of paper as a dollar bill? Of course not! At least, not if you've ever seen a real dollar bill. You know what a dollar bill looks like and feels like. You know that dollar bills are green—not purple!

In today's world, however, people fall for counterfeit ideas about the spiritual world all the time that are worth about as much as a purple dollar bill. They fall for counterfeits because they don't know what the real thing looks like. They don't know that they can find the truth about the spiritual world in the Bible.

Over the next few weeks your child will be part of a group that will explore the spiritual world—or what we will be calling the "invisible world." We will take a hard look at everything from angels to the afterlife. We will ask the students what they've heard about these things from their friends and from the media, and we will ask them what they think about it. But most important, we will encourage students to ask, "What does the Bible say about that?"

Your children are just now beginning to think in abstract ways—they are just now learning that something can be "invisible" to human eyes, yet still be real. While they try to figure out what they believe about the invisible world, they are bombarded with a barrage of spiritual information and misinformation every day. It is important that they learn they have a "Truth Source" where they

Unit Verse:

John 17:17b—*"Your word is truth."*

Unit Affirmation:

I CAN USE THE BIBLE TO JUDGE WHAT'S TRUE ABOUT THE INVISIBLE WORLD.

can go to to learn what's true and what's counterfeit about the invisible world. That truth source is the Bible.

Bank tellers and Secret Service agents learn to identify counterfeit bills not by studying counterfeits but by handling the real thing. When we study the invisible world in this unit, that's exactly what we'll do. We will study the *real thing*—what God's Word says as recorded in the Bible.

Principles

In this unit, your children will learn the Secret Service Agent's Motto for learning the truth about the invisible world and identifying counterfeits. This motto consists of the following three principles. Review the principles with your children.

PRINCIPLE #1
I CAN FIND THE TRUTH IN THE BIBLE

Your children will learn that the Bible is our truth source. They will learn that since the Bible tells us what the "real thing" is when it comes to the spiritual world, it should be the first place we look when we have questions about spiritual things.

PRINCIPLE #2
I CAN IDENTIFY COUNTERFEITS

Your children will learn that they can identify counterfeit ideas about the spiritual world by comparing them to what the Bible has to say. Since the Bible is our truth source, we know that any idea presented in the media or by peers that contradicts the Bible is a counterfeit idea.

PRINCIPLE #3
I CAN USE THE TRUTH

It's one thing to know what the truth is. It's another to use it to bring honor to God. Your children will learn how to apply what the Bible says about the spiritual world to their own lives. For example, they will learn to pray with more confidence and power, knowing that angels are sent by God to serve and protect Christians. And they will learn that worshiping God, both now and in heaven, is one of the highest callings for followers of God.

pRaCtICe

1. Make a Date!
Pick a special time each day to have a "date" with your child. It doesn't have to take much time or money—a short walk will do. You can even squeeze "special time" for discussion out of a trip to soccer practice. Whatever time you can make to be alone, ask your child about what he or she is learning.

2. Be a Sounding Board.
Preteens trying to live a Christian life can expect to have their faith challenged by friends and even teachers. As they mature and step out on their own, they are more and more likely to come in contact with false teachings about concepts important to their faith, including the afterlife, angels, and the end of the world. They may have questions about things they see on TV or hear at school. It is important for you to be there as a sounding board and an example. Share with your children about your own commitment to the Lord. Let your children know that it is great that they ask these questions and try to learn more about the invisible world.

"Your
word
is truth."

John 17:17b

I Can Use the Bible to Judge What's True about the Invisible World

Lesson 1

The Truth Is in There

Aim: That your students will understand they can find the truth about the invisible world in the Bible.

Scripture: Matthew 4:1-11

Unit Verse: "Your word is truth." John 17:17b

Unit Affirmation: I CAN USE THE BIBLE TO JUDGE WHAT'S TRUE ABOUT THE INVISIBLE WORLD!

1 | Setting the Stage (5-10 minutes)

WHAT YOU'LL DO
- Identify a real dollar bill in a bag full of counterfeits.

WHAT YOU'LL NEED
- Paper strips cut from a variety of paper types (see Planning Ahead), brown paper bags, blindfolds, stickers, $1 bills

PLANNING AHEAD
- Cut out various kinds of paper the exact size of dollar bills. Use construction paper, drawing paper, paper from a brown bag, and so on

2 | Introducing the Issue (20 minutes)

WHAT YOU'LL DO
- Read a parable about people who had the truth but didn't use it.
- Introduce the idea that the truth can be found in God's Word.

WHAT YOU'LL NEED
- Copies of "The Land Where People Knew Nothing" Activity Sheet (page 15)
- Unit Poster

PLANNING AHEAD
- Make the Unit Poster (see directions on page 5 and poster on page 9).

3 | Searching the Scriptures (20 minutes)

WHAT YOU'LL DO
- Present Matthew 4:1-11 as a "live puppet show."
- Introduce and practice the Secret Service Agent's motto.

WHAT YOU'LL NEED
- Chalkboard, whiteboard, or newsprint; chalk or marker

4 | Living the Lesson (5-10 minutes)

WHAT YOU'LL DO
- Give students an opportunity to commit to reading the Bible.

WHAT YOU'LL NEED
- Copies of the "Truth Seeker's Covenant" Activity Sheet (page 16)

Lesson 1

✔ Setting the Stage (5-10 minutes)

Ahead of time, prepare several "counterfeit detection" stations. Fill small paper bags with strips of various kinds of paper, such as newsprint, construction paper, typing paper, lined paper, and paper cut from a brown bag. Cut each paper strip to the exact size of a one dollar bill. Add a real one dollar bill to each bag and mix well. Put one bag at each station.

As students arrive, send them to one of the stations. Challenge students to try to detect which is the real dollar bill at their station by using sense of touch and smell only. To do this, appoint one volunteer at each station to blindfold each guesser. Let each student have a turn. If a student correctly identifies the dollar, put a sticker on his or her shirt.

✔ Introducing the Issue (20 minutes)

You were looking for the fake dollar bills in your bag. What's another word for fake that's often used when we talk about phony money? (Counterfeit.)

Ask everyone with a sticker to stand up. **Congratulations! You found the real dollar bills. You detected the counterfeits! How did you do it? How did you tell which piece of paper was the real dollar bill?** Let a few students explain how they knew which piece of paper was the real dollar bill.

Which "counterfeits" were easiest to detect? Why? (Probably the construction paper because it felt thicker than a real dollar bill.)

Which "counterfeits" were hardest to detect? Why? (Probably the bill cut from a brown paper bag because it felt and smelled like a real dollar bill.)

People who make counterfeit money work hard to make their bills as close to the real thing as they can. It's a tough job to detect the counterfeits. Does anyone know the name of the people whose job it is to detect counterfeits? (Secret Service agents.)

Does anyone know how Secret Service agents do it? How do they tell counterfeits from the real thing? Supplement students' responses with the following information: **Secret Service agents don't spend a lot of time studying counterfeits. Most of their training is studying the real thing. The better they know what a real dollar bill looks, smells, and feels like, the better they are at identifying imitations and fakes of the real thing.**

Money isn't the only thing that can be counterfeit. Let's think for a minute about the invisible world, the world that exists that we can't see. Another name for the invisible world is the "spiritual" world and it includes God, angels, heaven, and hell, among other things. Are there such things as counterfeits in the invisible world? Sure there are! There are counterfeit gods, phony religions, bogus ideas about heaven and hell, and

all kinds of notions about the spiritual world that are simply not true. But how do you know which ideas are counterfeits and which ideas are real? How do you know what the truth is about the invisible world? Over the next few weeks, we're going to go through some important training. We're all going to become Secret Service agents of the invisible world. When we're done with our training, we'll begin to be able to identify spiritual truth from spiritual counterfeits.

Pass out copies of "The Land Where People Knew Nothing" Activity Sheet. Read the story together or give students time to read it on their own. **What do you think of the Know Nothings who had The Book that contained all the truth, yet they kept looking "out there" for the truth?**

How is the Land Where People Knew Nothing like our own world? Do you know anyone who seems to always be looking for the truth but never finding it? Have you ever heard anyone say, "The truth is out there"? What does that mean?

We don't want to be like the Know Nothings. We have a great resource for finding the truth—The Bible! We need to use it. Display the Unit Poster and read the Unit Verse together. **The Bible is God's Word to us. Because God, through His Holy Spirit, helped people write the Bible, we can be sure that what it says is true. We can use the Bible to judge what's true about the invisible world.** Repeat the Unit Affirmation together: I CAN USE THE BIBLE TO JUDGE WHAT'S TRUE ABOUT THE INVISIBLE WORLD! **Do you remember how Secret Service agents are able to identify counterfeits? Because they know what the real thing looks like. The Bible tells us what the "real things" are concerning the invisible world.**

✔ Searching the Scripture (20 minutes)

Satan thinks he's pretty good at making spiritual counterfeits. In fact, he thinks he's so good at it that he even tried his counterfeit ideas on Jesus! We can learn a lot about spotting spiritual counterfeits by watching how Jesus exposed Satan's counterfeits.

Explain that you will hold a "live puppet show." Assign two students to be the "puppets," one representing Jesus, the other Satan. Divide the rest of the class into two teams, one team that will pose Jesus, the other that will pose Satan.

Ask a student to read Matthew 4:1-2. Explain that Satan's confrontation with Jesus was like a battle or a fight. Satan made some offers that sounded good at first, but they were counterfeit offers and not as good as the real thing. Jesus knew Satan was trying to deliver a knock-out punch. Jesus both protected Himself and fought back by using Scripture. Tell both teams to pose the students playing Jesus and Satan as if they were boxers, squaring off in a ring with their "dukes up." To make the poses, students can move arms and

legs into the positions they want. The students playing Jesus and Satan should cooperate and hold the poses.

Have a student read Matthew 4:3. Have the Satan team pose Satan as if he was about to punch Jesus in the face. **Satan took his best shot at Jesus. Jesus wasn't fooled. Lets find out what He said.** Ask a student to read Matthew 4:4. Ask the Jesus team to pose Jesus blocking Satan's punch to His face. **How did Jesus defend Himself against Satan's attacks?** Flip your Bible to Deuteronomy 8:3, and read it aloud. **Jesus was quoting Scripture!** Hold up the Bible. **Jesus knew that the truth is in here. Even Jesus quoted Scripture when He was confronted with counterfeit ideas.**

Satan decided to try something else. He tried using Scripture himself, but he used it out of context. That means Satan pulled out just one little piece of the Bible and pretended it had a different meaning than it really did. Ask a student to read Matthew 4:5-6. Tell the Satan team to pose Satan as if he was about to undercut Jesus by kicking out His legs. Then read Matthew 4:7. **Jesus knew the Bible better than Satan.** Ask the Jesus team to pose Jesus as if He had grabbed Satan's leg in mid-air, defending Himself from Satan's kick.

Satan wasn't finished yet. Ask a student to read Matthew 4:8-9. Tell the Satan team to pose Satan this time lunging toward Jesus, about to tackle Him. **Again, Jesus used Scripture to defeat Satan.** Read Matthew 4:10-11. Have the Jesus team pose Jesus moving out of the way of Satan's lunge at Him. Have the Satan team pose Satan losing his balance and falling head first toward the floor. **Because He knew the Bible so well, Jesus defeated Satan.** Have the Satan team pose Satan lying face down on the floor. Have the Jesus team pose Jesus celebrating His victory with one foot on top of Satan's back. Invite students to cheer for Jesus' victory, then ask students to return to their seats.

Let's review: Jesus came prepared for His battle with Satan. How was Jesus prepared to face Satan and his counterfeits? (He was prepared with knowledge from the Bible.) **We want to be like Jesus. Before Satan tries to fool us with counterfeits, we want to be prepared. We can do that by studying the Bible.**

Write "1. I CAN FIND THE TRUTH IN THE BIBLE" on a chalkboard or piece of newsprint. **If we learn the Scripture like Jesus did, what will we also be able to do when we are faced with counterfeits?** (We will be able to find and believe the truth in the Bible.)

Write "2. I CAN IDENTIFY COUNTERFEITS." **The invisible world is a tough world to figure out. It's easy to be fooled by counterfeit religions or phony ideas about spiritual things. Have you ever asked questions like these: What really happens when you die? What about people like those "psychics" on TV who seem to have magical power but don't believe in God? What's the truth about angels? We're going to tackle all these questions over the next few weeks. Remember the two steps we've written**

down. These two steps are part of the Secret Service Agent's Motto. Each week we will follow these two steps to help us answer tough questions about the invisible world.

But there is a third step we must follow, too. It is our job—yours and mine—to show the world that what the Bible says about God and Jesus is the truth. We not only have to *know* the truth that's in the Bible, we have to *use* the truth in the Bible. One way we can do that is to tell others about the truth. Write "3. I CAN USE THE TRUTH" on the board.

✔ Living the Lesson (5-10 minutes)

Hold up your Bible. **The truth is in here. But if you are going to be a Secret Service agent—if you are going to learn how to detect Satan's counterfeits—it has to be in here** (point at you head), **too. It can't help you if this book is sitting on your dresser by your bed.** (Toss your Bible on the table.) **It can't help you if you are carrying it around under your arm.** (Snatch it up and march around with it under your arm.) **It can't even help you if you know a lot of people who know the truth, like your mom or dad or pastor. You have to know it yourself. It has to be in your head and in your heart. You have to read the Bible. You have to know what it says. And if you do, no counterfeit truth can trick you! I'm going to stand by the truth. I'm going to stand with Jesus. What about you?**

Pass out pencils and copies of the "Truth Seeker's Covenant" Activity Sheet. Some students are just beginning to get the place where they can take ownership of their own walk with Christ and the spiritual disciplines—like reading the Bible—that are a part of that walk. Ask students to take a few minutes to read over the commitment sheet and decide if they are ready to make a commitment to read their Bibles for a specific amount of time and at a specific time each week. Be sure that students know even a five-minute commitment per week is a good place to start.

Share about how you find time to read your Bible. Do you get up extra early? Have you had to give up something you liked in order to have time to spend reading your Bible?

Be sensitive to your students' needs. Some students may not even have a Bible. As you close in prayer, thank God for His power over the invisible world. Thank Him that He gives us the tools to defeat Satan and the desire to read His Word, the Bible. Pray that God will help the students read their Bibles more, to help them as they learn about the truths of the invisible world.

The Land Where People Knew Nothing

Once upon a time, there was a man. I don't know what his name was. Actually, *he* didn't even know his own name. In fact, this man didn't know anything! He had many bruises on his head because he didn't know how to walk and chew gum at the same time. And he often wore pink socks because he didn't know you're not supposed to wash red shirts and white socks in the washing machine together.

The Man Who Knew Nothing may seem weird to you but he really wasn't all that weird where he lived because he lived in the Land Where People Knew Nothing. Everyone was as strange as he was. The Know Nothings who lived in the Land Where People Knew Nothing all believed that the answers to everything they didn't know were "out there" somewhere. The Man Who Knew Nothing used to sit on his porch both day and night and stare into space, as if waiting for the answers to drop out of the sky.

One day, The Man Who Knew Everything came to visit the Land Where People Knew Nothing. The Man Who Knew Everything found a man sitting on his porch, repeating "The truth is out there . . . The truth is out there."

"What are you doing?" asked the Man Who Knew Everything.

"I don't know," said the Man Who Knew Nothing. (What else would you expect him to say?)

The more The Man Who Knew Everything spent time with the Know Nothings, the more he had compassion on their situation. He taught the Know Nothings as much he could. He even taught them how to walk and chew gum at the same time. Then, when it was time for The Man Who Knew Everything to leave, he wrote down answers to many of the Know Nothings' toughest questions in The Book. He wrote down answers to questions like: Where did we come from? What happens when we die? What's life all about, anyway? And, why do sales people always call right in the middle of dinner? He gave the Know Nothings The Book as a going-away gift.

The Know Nothings were so happy to have The Book that they wanted to keep it in the safest place possible. So they put it in a huge vault and locked it up. And they never read it.

Before long, the Know Nothings went back to doing what they always did. They just kept sitting on their front porches, staring at the sky, and waiting. Waiting for answers to questions like: Where did we come from? and What happens when we die? The Know Nothings never thought to actually open The Book and read it. They just kept repeating, "The truth is out there . . . the truth is out there."

© 1998 David C. Cook. Permission granted to reproduce for classroom use only.

✔ Truth Seeker's Covenant

I,_____ , believe that the Bible is God's Word.

I will read my Bible: _____
(fill in a time and place)

If I do not understand part of what I am reading, I will:

"Your word is truth."
John 17:17b

Signed, _____

this _____ day of _____ , _____
      day   *month*   *year*

© 1998 David C. Cook. Permission granted to reproduce for classroom use only.

16

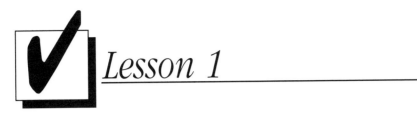

Notes

 *Lesson 2*

For Heaven's Sake!

Aim: That your students will understand what the Bible says about heaven and learn to identify "counterfeit" ideas about the afterlife.

Scripture: John 14:2-3; 1 Corinthians 15:42-44; Revelation 21:1-4; 22:1-4

Unit Verse: "Your word is truth." John 17:17b

Unit Affirmation: I CAN USE THE BIBLE TO JUDGE WHAT'S TRUE ABOUT THE INVISIBLE WORLD!

1 Setting the Stage

WHAT YOU'LL DO
- Buy tickets to one of two places based on what travel agents say.

WHAT YOU'LL NEED
- Copies of the Bulah and Iwanna Land tickets from the "Tickets to Paradise" Activity Sheet, lima beans
- Travel flyers, posters, and pictures
- OPTIONAL: Whistle or recording of a train whistle and CD/cassette player

PLANNING AHEAD
- Cut out copies of the "Tickets" Activity Sheet (page 24). Put the Heaven tickets aside for use in Living the Lesson.
- Set up your room like a travel agency.
- Prepare older students or volunteers to play the part of Travel Agents.

2 Introducing the Issue

WHAT YOU'LL DO
- Draw pictures that represent various beliefs about life after death.
- Discuss those beliefs.

WHAT YOU'LL NEED
- Drawing supplies (newsprint, markers, and crayons), stuffed animals, chalkboard
- Unit Poster

3 Searching the Scriptures

WHAT YOU'LL DO
- Make collages representing three key things the Bible says about heaven.
- Apply the Secret Service Agent's Motto to counterfeit ideas about heaven.

WHAT YOU'LL NEED
- Collage supplies (newsprint, old magazines and newspapers, scissors, tape or glue), chalkboard, or newsprint and marker

4 Living the Lesson

WHAT YOU'LL DO
- Discuss ways people try to "buy" tickets to heaven.
- Give students the opportunity to accept free tickets to heaven.

WHAT YOU'LL NEED
- Play money
- Copies of "Ticket to Heaven" cut out from the "Tickets to Paradise" Activity Sheet

Lesson 2

Setting the Stage (5-10 minutes)

Decorate your room like a travel agency. Post travel flyers, posters, and pictures around the room. Recruit two volunteers to be travel agents, one for a place called Bulah, the other for a place called Iwanna Land. Tell the travel agents to act like sales people, pitching their particular destinations. Equip each travel agent with a stack of tickets to his or her respective destination. (Cut out these tickets ahead of time from the "Tickets to Paradise" Activity Sheet.)

When students enter, give them each three lima beans and tell them that they have enough to buy one ticket to either Bulah or Iwanna Land, but not to both. Tell students to walk back and forth between the two agents to gather information. The first travel agent should describe Bulah as a tropical paradise featuring blue skies, sunny weather, and beautiful beaches. Travel agents may ad lib additional, similar details as needed. Tell the second travel agent to describe Iwanna Land as a winter wonderland featuring snow-covered trees, complimentary snowboarding, transportation by dog sled, etc.

For added fun, interrupt the activities periodically to give an update from travelers at both destinations. The reports from Bulah should continue to come in positively—weather is warm, people are enjoying the activities, etc. The reports from Iwanna Land should get progressively worse—the food is cold, the temperatures are dropping, a blizzard is on the way, etc.—until finally you say: **A traveler in Iwanna Land writes . . . this is a little hard to read, her writing is a little shaky . . . It says "Warning! Iwanna Land has no heat! No fire! Everything here is frozen! P.S. Get me outta here. I wanna go home!**

Leave a few seconds for any students who still have tickets for Iwanna Land to try to trade them in. But try to announce the final call (use the whistle) in time to "stick" at least one or two students with unwanted tickets to Iwanna Land.

Introducing the Issue (20 minutes)

Buying a ticket to someplace you've never seen is a little bit like trying to figure out what will happen after we die. If we've never been there, how do we know what it's like? Just as we did when we decided to buy a ticket for either Bulah or Iwanna Land, we must gather as much information as we can.

People have all kinds of ideas about what will happen after we die. What are some of the ideas that you've heard? Write as many ideas as students can come up with on a chalkboard or large sheet of newsprint.

Divide into three groups, pass out markers or crayons and a large piece of newsprint to each group, and make these assignments:

- Group 1: Draw an ocean. Just draw water—not people, sand, or fish.
- Group 2: Draw any and all kinds of animals you can think of.
- Group 3: Draw a number of dead people resting in coffins.

Explain that each group has just drawn a "travel poster" for one of the afterlife "destinations" many people believe in. Discuss these theories:

• ONE WITH THE UNIVERSE Theory—Refer to the "travel poster" of the ocean scene. **Some people believe that after you die you become "one with the universe." According to this theory, there is one great big "life force" and everything in the universe is a part of it. It's like this picture of the ocean. You're a part of the ocean. I'm a part of the ocean. Your dog and all the plants outside are all a part of this ocean.**

Discuss: **You have just one ticket to spend on your eternal destination. What would you think of this destination? Would you want to go here? Why or why not? What do you think it would be like to live for an eternity as part of a great ocean or light or life force knowing that you have no real personality or sense of self?**

• REINCARNATION theory— Refer to the "travel poster" of animals. **Some people believe in reincarnation.** Bring in a number of stuffed animals. Hold up the first stuffed animal. **They believe that after you die** (drop the first stuffed animal) **your soul will be born into another body here on earth** (hold up a different stuffed animal). **They say this process happens over and over again. You live and die hundreds of times and usually have no memory of your previous lives.** (While you read this, continue to rotate the stuffed animals, displaying each new animal for the audience.) **If you do good things in this life, you might come back as a dog or human. If you do bad things, you might end up as something undesirable, like a snail or mosquito.**

Discuss: **You just have one ticket to spend on your eternal destination. Would you want that destination to be reincarnation? Why or why not? What do you think it would be like to live for an eternity as one kind of animal then another and another but with no memory of your previous life?**

• NO AFTERLIFE AT ALL theory—Refer to the "travel poster" of people in coffins. **Still other people think there is no such thing as an afterlife. When you die, you die. You never wake up or reincarnate or go on to any kind of afterlife. You lose your consciousness and you never get it back.**

Discuss: **You just have one ticket to spend on your eternal destination. What would you think of this destination? Would you want to go here? Why or why not? What do you think it would be like to live for just a short while and know you would never experience any kind of afterlife?**

Of course, we know that we can't just decide to go where we *want* to when we die. But with all these theories, how can we know what really happens to us when we die? Display the Unit Poster and read the Unit Verse together. **Because God's Word—the Bible—is the truth, we can use the Bible to find out what's true about the afterlife.** Repeat the Unit Affirmation together.

Lesson 2

✔ Searching the Scripture (20 minutes)

The Bible describes a place called heaven where those who believe in Jesus go when they die. If we've only got one ticket to spend on our eternal destination doesn't it sound like a good idea to gather as much information as we can about heaven now? What's it like? Will it be fun or boring? How can we know? The Bible gives us beautiful glimpses of heaven, just like pictures in a travel guide.

Pass out new pieces of newsprint to each group. Pass out stacks of old magazines, scissors, invisible tape or glue, and crayons or markers. Give groups the following assignments:

- **Group 1:** Make a collage that represents a "dream house." What kind of furniture would you find in the house? Does it have a swimming pool or a basketball court in the back yard?
- **Group 2:** What if you had the chance to redesign the human body? Make a collage showing what the new body can do. Does it have 10 arms and 10 legs for more efficiency? Can it fly? What else can it do?
- **Group 3:** Make a collage of fun, exciting things to do.

Let Group 1 display and explain its picture of the ideal house. Then say: **This picture of an ideal house is sort of like a travel guide for heaven. But even the greatest house we could dream up living in here on earth is only a** *taste* **of the ideal house we will live in in heaven!** Read John 14:2-3. **These verses only tell us that Jesus prepared a place for us to live with Him in heaven. They don't tell us what it will be like. But we can trust Jesus. If He has made a place for us, we know that it will be better than any place the world has to offer. Heaven will even be better than the ideal house!** Write "BETTER PLACE" on the board.

Let Group 2 display and explain its picture of the "new and improved" human body. Then say: **These pictures of a new human body are also like a travel guide for heaven. The Bible promises that we will get new, perfect bodies that will even be better than the ideal bodies this group just described.**

Before reading 1 Corinthians 15:42-44, explain that Paul has been writing to the Corinthian church about something called the "resurrection of the dead," which has to do with us dying and then coming alive again in heaven with new bodies. Read the verses, then discuss: **Paul knows that the bodies that we have are perishable and going to die. He says, however, that if we have a relationship with Jesus, when we get to heaven we will receive new bodies that will not die.**

We don't know for sure, but what do you think our new bodies will look like? What kinds of things do you think we'll be able to do with our new bodies that we can't now? (Take responses.) **Even the most ideal body we can think of on earth will look weak compared to our bodies in heaven!** Write

"BETTER BODIES" on the board.

Let Group 3 display and explain its picture of fun things to do. Then say: **The pictures on this poster are also like a travel guide for heaven. But heaven is even better than this! The Bible says that if you can find fun things to do in this world, you will be even more excited and fulfilled in heaven.**

Have volunteers read Revelation 21:1-4 and 22:1-4. Then comment: **The Bible says that in heaven there will be no more death or mourning or crying or pain, and God Himself will wipe every tear from His children's eyes! God wants us to experience all of His glory, but that will only happen once we get to heaven. And this passage tells us that it will be so wonderful, and there will be no more tears or crying. It says that the "curse" that keeps us from seeing God in all His glory will be lifted. The Bible says over and over again that the most fulfilling, satisfying, and exciting thing we can ever do is relate to God and spend time in His awesome presence. It says that most of the good things that we do for fun or excitement are OK, but they pale in comparison to how fulfilling it is to be in God's presence. In our new bodies, when the "curse" is lifted, we will get all new desires. In a sense, we will get a whole new definition of what fun and excitement is. We will desire to be with God. And we will be able to be with God—for an eternity!** Write "BETTER RELATIONSHIP WITH GOD" on the board.

Now that we know some about what heaven's like according to the Bible, we can identify counterfeit ideas about the afterlife. Review the "Secret Service Agent's Motto." Help students remember the key phrases of the motto and write on the board:

1. I CAN FIND THE TRUTH IN THE BIBLE.
2. I CAN IDENTIFY COUNTERFEITS.
3. I CAN USE THE TRUTH.

✔ Living the Lesson (5-10 minutes)

Refer to the "travel poster" of the coffins some students made in Introducing the Issue and say: **The Bible tells us there is certainly an afterlife and it consists of either heaven or another eternal destination called hell. It doesn't say as much about hell as it does about heaven, but the Bible does say hell is real. In fact, Jesus Himself talked about hell more than anyone else in the New Testament. He called it a place of unquenchable fire (Mark 9:43). He said that hell is a place prepared for Satan and his demons (Matthew 25:41), but there will be people in hell, too.**

If we have a choice between two eternal destinations—heaven or hell, where would you rather go? If you *do* want to go to heaven, it would make sense for us to find out how the Bible says we can get to heaven, wouldn't it?

Lesson 2

Hold up a ticket to heaven (cut out from the "Tickets to Paradise" Activity Sheet). Discuss: **How much does a ticket to heaven cost? How can you get one? What are some ways people try to "buy" a ticket to heaven?**

God knew we could never be good enough or smart enough to *earn* a ticket to heaven. So God sent His Son, Jesus, to die on the cross for us. That way, all we have to do is admit that we are sinners and we need God's help. God offers this gift of grace and forgiveness to us free, and He wants us to trust Him so we can be in heaven with Him when we die.

Leave students time to pray silently. Invite some students to ask for Jesus' forgiveness and accept Jesus into their hearts for the first time. Encourage other students to spend some time thanking God for the sacrifice He made so they could spend eternity with Him in heaven. Be on the lookout for students who may be praying to accept Jesus for the first time. Invite them to stay after class to discuss the decision they've made.

ADMISSION to
Bulah

ADMISSION to
Iwanna Land

ADMISSION to
Heaven

© 1998 David C. Cook. Permission granted to reproduce for classroom use only.

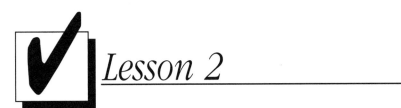

Notes

Lesson 3

Touched by Angels

Aim: That your students will understand what the Bible says about angels and learn how to identify "counterfeit" ideas about angels.

Scripture: Hebrews 1:14; Psalm 91:9-12
Unit Verse: "Your word is truth." John 17:17b
Unit Affirmation: I CAN USE THE BIBLE TO JUDGE WHAT'S TRUE ABOUT THE INVISIBLE WORLD!

1 Setting the Stage

WHAT YOU'LL DO
- Create imaginary creatures from pictures of humans, animals, insects, and machines.

WHAT YOU'LL NEED
- Three brown paper bag, various magazine clippings representing all types of animals, machines, men, and women (see Planning Ahead), construction paper, glue, scissors; crayons or markers

PLANNING AHEAD
- Cut out a variety of pictures from magazines representing all types of animals. Also cut out various pictures of machines, men, and women.
- Cut the pictures apart, separating the head, arms, legs, and body of each creature, machine, or person.
- Mix the picture parts together and put them in three brown paper bags.

2 Introducing the Issue

WHAT YOU'LL DO
- Take a true/false quiz about angels.

WHAT YOU'LL NEED
- Copies of "A Heavenly Quiz" Activity Sheet (page 31)
- Unit Poster

3 Searching the Scriptures

WHAT YOU'LL DO
- Unscramble key words about angels.
- Identify three key characteristics of angels.

WHAT YOU'LL NEED
- Word Bags (see Planning Ahead)

PLANNING AHEAD
- Write the words "SPIRIT," "SERVE," and "STRONG" in large letters on a piece of paper.
- Make four photocopies of this paper, then cut out each individual letter.
- Prepare the four word bags by putting a set of all the letters that spell "SPIRIT," "SERVE," and "STRONG" into each of those bags.

4 Introducing the Issue

WHAT YOU'LL DO
- Practice praying for God's help.

WHAT YOU'LL NEED
- Copies of "Practical Prayers" Activity Sheet (page 32)

Lesson 3

✔ Setting the Stage (5-10 minutes)

Ahead of time, set up three Creation Stations. Cut a variety of animal pictures out of magazines. Also cut out various pictures of machines, men, and women. Cut the pictures apart, separating the head, body, and legs of each creature, person, or machine. Mix the picture parts together and put them in brown paper bags. Place one bag at each of the activity stations. Also put construction paper, glue, scissors, and crayons or markers at each station.

When students arrive, send each to one of the activity stations with these directions: **Have you ever wondered if there are any other intelligent creatures in the universe? And if there are, what would they look like? Use the parts in the bag to build your own creature!** In addition to gluing various clippings from their bags onto their paper, students can draw features onto their pictures if they wish. Have students share their creations.

✔ Introducing the Issue (20 minutes)

How many movies and TV shows can you think of about strange creatures coming to earth? Let the students brainstorm answers. Count the number of movies and TV shows they can come up with that deal with alien visitors.

Our culture seems to be fascinated by the idea of strange creatures visiting our world. In fact, right now scientists around the world are searching the skies with radio telescopes, hoping to hear a signal that would mean they had found intelligent life *out there somewhere.* **At one time or another most people have wondered: Are we alone in the universe? Are there any other intelligent life forms out there? Can we communicate with them?** Pick up one of the creature pictures. **What do they look like?**

What if I told you that people have been around intelligent creatures ever since . . . well, ever since Adam and Eve? The creatures are angels—and they are very real. The Bible mentions angels 273 times! Can you think of anything that angels did in the Bible? Take a few responses.

Pass out pencils and copies of the "A Heavenly Creature Quiz" Activity Sheet. Read each question and let the students circle true or false. Discuss: **Are people at your school interested in angels? What do most people at your school think about angels? Have any of you ever heard stories of people being helped by angels?** Your students may come up with some off-the-wall stories, but don't worry. The truth about what angels do and don't do will be covered thoroughly in this lesson. This question will get students talking.

On the one hand, many people refuse to believe that angels exist. On the other hand, more and more people these days seem to be talking about some strange ideas about angels. Some people claim that angels are their

special spirit guides; still others say that angels come from different planets. **Which ideas are true and which are counterfeit?** Display the Unit Poster and read the Unit Verse together. **Because God's Word—the Bible—is the truth, we can use the Bible to find out what's true about angels.** Repeat the Unit Affirmation together.

✔ Searching the Scripture (20 minutes)

Ahead of time, write the words "SPIRIT," "SERVE," and "STRONG," in large letters on a piece of paper. Make four photocopies of this paper, then cut out each individual letter. Prepare eight "word bags." Prepare the first set of four word bags by putting a set of all the letters that spell "SPIRIT," "SERVE," and "STRONG" into each bag.

Divide into four groups. Give each group one of the first set of word bags. **There are 17 letters in your bag that can be unscrambled to spell three words. All three words describe something important about angels. You can find clues to help you figure out these words by reading Hebrews 1:14. When I say go, find and read this Bible verse. Then dump out your letters on the ground and see if you can unscramble them to spell the three key angel words. Ready? Go!**

For the first word, "SPIRIT," ask for a volunteer. When the student is chosen, have him or her stand in front of the group. **We have a volunteer here who is going to show us what it is like to be a "Spirit statue."** Ask the class to help you decide how to best represent spirit in a "living statue." This will be difficult precisely because a spirit is not a physical entity. This fact may, however, generate interesting conversation. After you have posed the student, have him or her stay that way. Explain: **Because angels are spirit beings, they are not limited to physical bodies like we are. Sometimes the people in the Bible saw the angels who were helping them, and sometimes they didn't. At times in the Bible angels took a human form to communicate with humans. At other times, they looked something like humans, only they were incredibly brilliant or beautiful. But most of the time, angels carry out their jobs in the invisible world. Most of the time we can't even see angels.**

For the second word, "SERVE," call on another volunteer and have the class decide what statue pose works best for someone who serves.

Explain: **God is the Boss of angels. That means angels serve God. What kinds of assignments, or jobs, does God give angels?** Review this information: God puts angels in charge of protecting Christians and giving people messages from God. You might mention some of the many stories in the Bible about angels helping people who believe in God: God sent angels with messages to Daniel, Zechariah, Mary, Joseph, shepherds, the women at the tomb, the

apostles, Philip, Cornelius, and John. Angels protected Lot from the Sodomites and Elisha from the Syrians, and they are still protecting God's people today.

For the third word, "STRONG," have a third volunteer stay in a pose for "strong" like he or she is a statue. Explain: **No matter whether the angels are invisible or appear visible for our benefit, they are always powerful. The Bible tells us in 2 Kings 19 that when the Assyrian army attacked Jerusalem, King Hezekiah asked God for help—and God sent one angel to help. Just one angel struck the Assyrian army—and 185,000 soldiers were lying dead on the field when the sun came up. How do you feel knowing you have such strong spiritual servants working to protect you?**

Isn't that amazing? God created incredibly strong spirit beings who live in the invisible world to help and protect us! Have someone read Psalm 91:9-12. Thank your statue volunteers and have them return to their seats.

We discussed some things that angels are. Now we need to discuss some things that angels are not. When you see things on TV or hear stories about them at school that are different than how the Bible describes angels, you can identify counterfeits. To help the students do this, have them get out their "Heavenly Creature Quiz" and review the following answers.

1. False. Explain: **Most of these incredibly powerful spirit beings worship God and do His will. But not all angels are God's servants any more. The Bible indicates that a powerful angel we call Satan rebelled against God. He apparently convinced one third of the heavenly host to fight on his side (Revelation 12:4, 9). We'll talk more about this angel and his army of fallen angels next week.**

2. False. Many times angels appeared on earth as men. The Bible never calls an angel "she." Of course, since angels are spirit beings, they are truly neither male nor female, so gender is not a significant issue (see Matthew 22:30).

3. True. The Bible never describes the angels who came to earth as having wings. (We do know they fly.) But in Ezekiel's and other visions of heaven, cherubim and seraphim are described as having wings, so at least some angels have wings.

4. True. Sometimes angels choose to appear to men and women this way.

5. False. Physical encounters with angels may be rare, but reliable Christians continue to report amazing stories about their encounters with angels to this day.

6. False. Nothing in the Bible even remotely implies this.

7. False. The Bible describes angels and humans as completely different species of God's creation.

8. True. As already read in Psalm 91:9-12 and other Scriptures.

9. True. See Genesis 18:1-7.

10. True. See Luke 2:13, 15:10; Hebrews 1:6.

11. True. See Luke 20:36.

✔ Living the Lesson (5-10 minutes)

We've learned a lot about God's messengers, His angels. **Now how can we use the truth we've learned?** Supplement students' responses by saying: **One of the best ways we can use this truth is to PRAY! Since we know that angels can protect us, we can pray to God and know that God will take care of us—whether He uses angels or some other means.**

Pass out copies of the "Practical Prayers" Activity Sheet. **This sheet will help you practice how you can pray to God during your day.** Tell students they can work on this sheet alone, in pairs, or in groups of three.

Instead of reviewing what students' wrote, you might choose to share some practical prayers that you have prayed recently in the middle of a given day. What did you pray while you were preparing for this lesson? What did you pray when you experienced a conflict at work? If you can, share how God answered those prayers in small and big ways.

Close with a time of "popcorn prayer." While students' eyes are shut and their heads are bowed, give them sentences to complete as prayers to God. Tell students they might complete the sentence with one word or many words. Be sure they know no one *has* to pray and that there is no order to the prayer. Use these sentence-starters or introduce your own: **I'm glad you created angels because. . . ,** and **I pray for protection for. . . .**

A Heavenly Creature Quiz

How much do you know about celestial, or heavenly beings?

If the statement is true, circle T. If it is false, circle F.

1. *All angels are good.*   **T   F**

2. *There are female angels.*   **T   F**

3. *Some angels have wings.*   **T   F**

4. *Angels look like humans, only bigger and kind of shiny.*   **T   F**

5. *Angels don't appear on earth any more.*   **T   F**

6. *When people die, they become angels.*   **T   F**

7. *A person can come back to earth as an angel.*   **T   F**

8. *There are angels watching over believers.*   **T   F**

9. *Angels can eat human food.*   **T   F**

10. *Angels experience emotion.*   **T   F**

11. *Angels never die.*   **T   F**

© 1998 David C. Cook. Permission granted to reproduce for classroom use only.

Practical Prayers ✔

You are walking home from school and suddenly you realize that the leaves are gold, the sky is ice blue, and the whole world seems to be shouting out how great God is . . . *What kind of prayer would you pray?*

You are wearing your best pair of jeans. You hop onto the school bus and plop into a seat—right on top of a big fat gob of gum . . . *What kind of prayer would you pray?*

Your best friend has a problem and asks you for advice . . . *What kind of prayer would you pray?*

You are sitting in your favorite restaurant and an ambulance races by . . . *What kind of prayer would you pray?*

It has been a totally terrific day and you are just about to drift off to sleep . . . *What kind of prayer would you pray?*

© 1998 David C. Cook. Permission granted to reproduce for classroom use only.

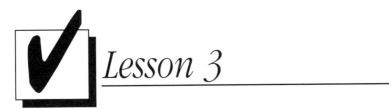

Notes

Lesson 4

Junk Power

Aim: That your students will understand what the Bible says about God's supernatural powers and learn to identify "counterfeit" supernatural powers that don't honor God.

Scripture: 1 Samuel 28:12-18; Deuteronomy 18:9-13

Unit Verse: "Your word is truth." John 17:17b

Unit Affirmation: I CAN USE THE BIBLE TO JUDGE WHAT'S TRUE ABOUT THE INVISIBLE WORLD!

1 Setting the Stage

WHAT YOU'LL DO
- Compete in Goof Ball Olympics (three games that use ping-pong balls)

WHAT YOU'LL NEED
- Ping-pong balls with faces on them, blocks, paper cups, balloons, paper sack

PLANNING AHEAD
- Make "Goof Balls" by drawing goofy faces on ping-pong balls

2 Introducing the Issue

WHAT YOU'LL DO
- Play a game to demonstrate how some "psychics" convince people they are real

WHAT YOU'LL NEED
- Quarter or other coin
- Unit Poster

3 Searching the Scriptures

WHAT YOU'LL DO
- Write "Believe It or Not" accounts about some of God's miracles
- Apply the Secret Service Agent's Motto to identifying supernatural powers

WHAT YOU'LL NEED
- Copies of the "Believe It or Not!" Activity Sheet (page 39), pencils

4 Living the Lesson

WHAT YOU'LL DO
- Write/draw an ending to a story about a kid whose friends are playing with a Ouija board.
- Brainstorm ways we can "hang tough for the truth."

WHAT YOU'LL NEED
- Copies of the "Hanging Tough for the Truth" Activity Sheet (page 40), pencils

 *Lesson 4*

✔ Setting the Stage (5-10 minutes)

Make a number of "goof balls": Using markers, draw smiley faces on a ping-pong balls. The "goofier" the faces the better. Set up and explain the directions to the three games below. Let students rotate from station to station as time allows. Appoint one adult or student volunteer to lead each station.

- **Maze Masters:** Make a "maze" of blocks on a table or desk. Each contestant tries to blow a goof ball off the opponent's side of the table.
- **Rocket Races:** Tape a large bull's-eye (three concentric octagons, for example) on a wall, then mark off a starting line 10 feet away. Each contestant blows up a balloon and holds the balloon closed without tying it. Other students help the contestant attach a goof ball to the nose of the balloon with a loop of tape. Contestants launch their rockets at the wall. The rocket that hits closest to the bull's-eye wins.
- **Truth or Consequences:** Write "T" on the bottom of nine paper cups and "F" on the bottom of nine more; set these right side up and close together on top of a small table. Make simple true or false statements such as, "The sun is hot." Let the contestant next in line bounce his or her goof ball off the table and into one of the cups. If it lands in the cup with the wrong answer or misses all the cups altogether, snatch the ball up and send the contestant to one of the other two stations. If it lands in a cup with the correct answer, give the goof ball back to that student and send him or her to the back of the line. Keep playing until all but one student is eliminated.

✔ Introducing the Issue (20 minutes)

Discuss: **Was there any skill involved in winning in the Goof Ball Olympics?** (A little; it was mostly luck, though.) **Which game involved the most skill? Why? Which game involved the most luck? Why?**

Hold up the goof ball that won the "Truth or Consequences" game. **This is the luckiest goof ball in the world. He won the Truth or Consequences game! Congratulations, Mr. Goof!** Make the goof ball nod by rolling it in your fingers, then stick him in your pocket. Cup your hands and whisper loudly, **I don't think it was his brains, though. That guy's head is full of air!**

Pull the goof ball out of your pocket. **Some people treat what they believe about the invisible world like they were playing a game in the Goof Ball Olympics. They don't take the time to find the truth. They throw their ball up in the air. Maybe they get lucky and it lands on the truth. Maybe they don't. People like this are willing to try anything and believe anything. You would think their heads were full of air!** Toss the goof ball in the air and let it bounce on the ground. **Do you want to live like that?**

Let's have one more contest to show how silly it is to treat our beliefs about the invisible world like a game of chance. **What's a psychic? Have you ever seen a psychic? What do psychics claim to be able to do?** (Tell the future.)

Lots of people believe in psychics. I have even seen people on TV claiming they used a psychic, and the psychic was right about what he or she predicted. Why do you think people believe in psychics?

Some so-called psychics are just good guessers—or they guess so many times that they have to get things right some of the time. I can show you how this works. Divide into two teams—the "Heads" team and the "Tails" team. Tell students you will flip a coin; if it lands heads, all the members of the Heads team get to take one step forward and all the Tails are out, or vice verse. Pull a quarter from your pocket. **Now, before I flip this coin, I am going to make a prediction.** Press your fingers to your temples and squint. **You . . . are . . . going to take one step forward!** Flip the coin; winners take one step forward, losers sit down. Repeat, having the students number off again and making the same prediction. Continue until there is just one student left, your winner. **Now, if I was pretending to be a psychic, which group of people do you think might believe me? The group that sat down first? How about the group that sat down next-to-last? How about the winner? My "predictions" were 100 percent accurate for him or her—but they were just guesses!** Have the class sit down. **That's how some psychics work. They guess enough times so that some of the time they're bound to be right. Can you see how silly it would be to just believe in any idea that's out there? Don't we need a better way of determining what's true about supernatural powers?**

Display the Unit Poster and read the Unit Verse together. **Since God's Word, the Bible, is true, we can use the Bible to judge what's true about things like supernatural powers.** Repeat the Unit Affirmation together a number of times.

✔ Searching the Scripture (20 minutes)

A lot of people claim to have "supernatural" power—that means they claim to be able to do things that other people can't. These people claim to get their power from the spiritual world. Many people claim that they have seen supernatural things happen in their lives. Some of these people may be fakes. In the game we just played, I was a "fake" psychic. But not all people who claim to have supernatural powers are fakes. **Do you believe that there are supernatural powers at work in this world or not?**

Pass out pencils, paper, and copies of the "Believe It or Not" Activity Sheet (page 39). Have students write accounts of the stories as directed on the sheet. Discuss: **Do you believe God can do supernatural, powerful things like the Bible says He did in these stories? Why or why not?**

Lesson 4

We talked about "fake" power, which is when people like phony psychics claim to have power they don't really have. And we've talked about God's power, which is the real thing. But there's another kind of power we need to talk about—Junk Power. Junk Power is to God's Power what junk food is to real food. **What are some examples of junk food?** (Candy, soda pop, etc.) **Do you feel full when you eat junk food?** (Usually, because it has a lot of calories.) **But does it give your body the nutrition it needs?** (No, that's why it's called "junk" food.) **What happens when you eat a lot of junk food?** (You may get sick. You're not as healthy as you would be if you ate good food.) **What would happen if you only ate junk food and never ate any real food?** (Your body would get almost no nutrition; you might get very sick and eventually die.)

Junk power is like junk food. Junk power comes from Satan, not from God. Like junk food, it may seem good and it may be fun at first. But junk power takes your focus off of God. And when you're not focused on God, you're not getting what you need to grow spiritually. People who mess with Satan's power can become spiritually sick and caught up in any number of things that will end up being very bad for them.

Review the Secret Service Agent's Motto. Write "I CAN FIND THE TRUTH IN THE BIBLE" on the board. Say: **Let's compare Satan's power, "Junk Power," with God's power, the Real Thing. Why does God work miracles and wonders, or give spiritual gifts to people?** (God uses His power to build up believers and to bring glory to Himself.)

It's hard to get tired of reading about the miracles in the Bible. It's amazing to think about how great and mighty our God is! All of His people love to hear about the miracles He has done. It gives them courage, and it helps keep their faith strong in times of trouble. In fact, people everywhere love to hear about God's supernatural power. But often, Satan tries to use this interest to lead people away from God.

Read 1 Samuel 28:12-18. **We know that Samuel had already outlawed mediums and witches and other people who tried to contact the dead. Why do you think he outlawed them?** (It was against God's law to practice such things; the power of these mediums come from Satan.)

If Saul outlawed witches and mediums, why did he seek out one himself? (He was desperate. His army was about to be defeated by the enemy Philistines, and God was not helping him anymore because Saul had been unfaithful to God in the past.)

What do you think God thinks of these counterfeits? Ask a student to read Deuteronomy 18:9-13. **God calls all of these things detestable! He warned His people against them thousands of years ago . . . and yet they are still with us today. What was once known as a medium is sometimes called a channeler now. Astrology and many kinds of fortunetelling are divination and interpreting omens. Psychics, healers, and people who**

perform "miracles" today without the power of God and not in the name of Christ are doing the very same things that the sorcerers and witches did in the Bible! Satan is still using the same old counterfeits—he has just given them new names.

People who experiment with occult practices can contact Satan's evil spirits. But experimentation with these spirits is very dangerous! You might start out playing games only to find out later you are trapped by Satan's power. Experimenting in the occult can lead a person to being controlled and even possessed by evil spirits. The Bible is very, very stern in its warnings to stay away from this kind of supernatural power. God hates any games or activities that invite Satan or evil spirits to work in your life.

Why would Satan want to trick people into becoming involved in psychic phenomenon, fortunetelling, sorcery, or magic? People today who depend on fortune tellers, astrology, or space aliens to save the world are not depending on God, are they?

Write "I CAN IDENTIFY COUNTERFEITS" on the board. Tell students to make a list of all the supernatural things they've ever heard of happening. Write this list down on the board. Then review: **Which of these things builds up believers by strengthening their faith and brings glory to God? Which one gives glory to humans, some kind of "spirit,'" or even Satan?** Make two columns on the board or your paper. Write "The Real Thing" over one and "Junk Power" over the other. Discuss your list and decide to put each item in one column or the other.

When God does something supernatural in our lives, it's an awesome thing! You will probably face many counterfeits. But you can remember to ask these questions about any supernatural power you see or experience: Does it bring honor to God or honor to Satan? And does it help or hurt people in the long run?

✔ Living the Lesson (5-10 minutes)

Pass out copies of the "Hanging Tough for the Truth" Activity Sheet. In this sheet, a student is confronted with an opportunity to dabble in an occult practice, the Ouija board. Give students a few minutes to complete the sheet as directed by drawing a possible ending to the scenario. Let as many students share their endings as you have time for. Discuss: **What are some other situations you might encounter where you might be invited to get involved with Satan's powers? What can you do in those situations?**

When you close in prayer, model for students how to pray with power for Jesus' protection and victory over Satan. Let students add their own one-sentence prayers if you wish.

Believe It or Not!

You have just been given a job as an ace reporter—for *Ripleyoboam's Bible Times Believe it Or Not!* YOUR ASSIGNMENT: Sharpen your pencils, look up each of these amazing events, and write an account for Believe It Or Not!

1. *Exodus 4:6-12*

2. *Numbers 22:20-35*

3. *1 Kings 17:2-6*

4. *Matthew 14:25*

5. *Daniel 3:19-25*

6. *1 Kings 18:25-39*

7. *2 Kings 6:1-7*

8. *Exodus 14:21-31*

© 1998 David C. Cook. Permission granted to reproduce for classroom use only.

Hanging Tough for the Truth

It's a dark and stormy night. Jana, a Christian, is spending the night at her cousin's birthday party. Suddenly...

How can Jana hang tough for the truth?
Draw a possible ending for this story.

© 1998 David C. Cook. Permission granted to reproduce for classroom use only.

Notes

 *Lesson 5*

The Final Chapter

Aim: That your students will understand that God is in control of future events and He has already won the war with Satan.

Scripture: Matthew 24:3-14, 36-42; Acts 2:17-21; Revelation 19:11-24; and Titus 2:11-14

Unit Verse: "Your word is truth." John 17:17b

Unit Affirmation: I CAN USE THE BIBLE TO JUDGE WHAT'S TRUE ABOUT THE INVISIBLE WORLD!

1 Setting the Stage

WHAT YOU'LL DO

- Illustrate pictures depicting Scripture about the end times.

WHAT YOU'LL NEED

- Newsprint, markers, crayons, and other drawing supplies as needed

2 Introducing the Issue

WHAT YOU'LL DO

- Discuss current headlines and the fears students might have about the end times.

WHAT YOU'LL NEED

- Newspapers or magazines
- Unit Poster

3 Searching the Scripture

WHAT YOU'LL DO

- Discuss and draw symbols of the signs Jesus told us to watch for.

WHAT YOU'LL NEED

- Mural paper, copies of the "Signs of the Times" Activity Sheet (page 46)

4 Living the Lesson

WHAT YOU'LL DO

- Fill out an activity sheet about what to do while we wait for Jesus' return.

WHAT YOU'LL NEED

- Copies of the "A Few Things To Do While We Wait" Activity Sheet (page 47)

Lesson 5

✔ Setting the Stage (5-10 minutes)

Set up four Illustration Stations by putting pencils, paper, crayons, and markers at each station. Ahead of time, write the following Scripture references each on its own index card and put one index card at each station also: Matthew 24:3-14, 36-42; Acts 2:17-21; Revelation 19:11-24; and Titus 2:11-14. When students arrive, send them to one of the four stations and explain that each student's job is to add pictures to the verses at the stations. Encourage them to add details and make the characters as authentic as possible. As the students draw, walk around from group to group and discuss the pictures. When the murals are done (or you run out of time), hang them up around the room.

✔ Introducing the Issue (20 minutes)

Ahead of time, bring in current newspapers or magazines. Hold up some of the headlines in your papers or magazines and read them aloud. **There are a lot of terrible things happening in the world today. Have you ever heard anyone say, "If there is a loving God, then why would He allow wars and famine and crime? Why wouldn't He just put a stop to it all?" The answer is easy: He will. But He has let the world go on because He loves you and me.**

Many people think we are getting close to the time when Jesus will come back. Some people call this the "end times." In fact, many people watch current events as a way to tell if Jesus is coming back soon. What do you think of this?

What kinds of things have you heard about the end times? Do you think we might be living in the end times? Take a few moments to explore your students' thoughts and fears. Let the students bring up the subjects that concern them, and discuss each one. They will often have worries such as "What if I get the mark of the beast by accident?" and "What if a rapture happens and I am left behind?" Are their concerns biblical? Christians living in the end times will need courage and faith—but even if we aren't living in the end times we need strength, faith, and courage to walk with Jesus! Assure them of God's faithfulness to His people, and remind them that His angels are watching over them.

Pass out copies of the Unit Poster. Read the Unit Verse together. **Because God's Word—the Bible—is truth, we can use the Bible to determine what's true about the end of the world.** Repeat the Unit Affirmation together.

✓ Searching the Scripture (20 minutes)

Imagine that you are on your way to Denver, Colorado. You are zipping down the highway, and everything looks the same for mile after mile. You don't seem to be getting any closer to your destination. Sure, you know that you will get there eventually. But when? And then you pass a sign. It says "Denver, 432 miles." It flashes past, and then roadside is going by, just like it did before. It doesn't seem to change at all, and it feels like you will never get there. Suddenly, you pass another sign. This one says "Denver, 370 miles." You know that you are getting closer! Jesus told His disciples to watch for signs—not road signs, but things that would happen before the end times. What Jesus told them is so important that I want to read it to you from the Bible. Listen carefully. Read Matthew 24:3-14. **What are the signs Jesus said to watch for?** Point out any of the signs that are in the headlines of magazines or newspapers today.

Do you think this could be the end times? Draw a timeline on a large piece of mural paper. Make a dot at one end of the line and an arrow at the other. Draw a vertical line through your "timeline" about one inch behind the arrow. **This dot is the day that God created Adam and Eve. This slash is 1900, just about a hundred years ago. Now if you counted all of the people who lived before 1900,** (drag your finger along the line all the way back to the beginning) **and then you counted all of the people who are alive today,** (go back to the other end, and measure the inch with your finger) **which number do you think would be greater? All the people who have lived and died, or all the people alive on earth today?** Let the class guess. The truth is, there are more people living in this little piece of our time line than lived in all time, back to Adam and Eve. **Could this be the harvest Jesus was talking about? All the people who are alive today? If so, that would be very exciting. Even if it is not the end of the age, it's our job to tell all these people about Jesus. We should be excited that we might be living in the end times—the time before Christ returns. But we should also be careful about what we hope and expect.** Direct your class's attention to each mural as you read the Scriptures from the Bible in this order: Matthew 26:36-42. **We will never know the exact day and hour when Jesus will return. But Jesus tells us to keep watch!**

What are some of the signs of the end times? Read Acts 2:17-21. **God will do amazing things, and He will pour out His Spirit on His people. Christians will take the good news about Jesus to the ends of the world! There will be very hard times for Christians.** NOTE: You'll want to point out to students that according to this passage, we are already living in the end times, at least in one sense. This passage was fulfilled at least partially by the fact that the Holy Spirit was poured out on believers at the Pentecost, and He continues to reside in believers today.

Lesson 5

The Bible tells us that the end times will be like no other time that ever has been or ever will be. No matter what happens on earth we know one thing for sure: Jesus has already won the battle. He won it when He died on the cross. The only reason He has allowed the world to go on this long is that He wants everyone to have an opportunity to come to God. And in the end, when God harvests the earth, Satan will be captured and bound up. Read Revelation 19:11-24.

Read Titus 2:11-14. **The most important event we have to look forward to about the very end times is the return of Christ. Christ will come back and announce what is called the "blessed hope" of the Christian.**

What does Titus 2:11-14 emphasize because Christians know that Christ is coming? (Live godly lives while we wait for Jesus to return.)

Pass out copies of the "Signs of the Times" Activity Sheet. Have students review what they just learned by drawing pictures of the "signs" God promises He will give us that Jesus is coming back soon. Ask for a few volunteers to share their signs with the class. **Even if we don't know the time and the date, God does. And we've seen that there is no one more powerful in the invisible world, and no one more powerful in the visible world than God. And that's how we know that no matter what happens in the future, God will always be in control.**

✔ Living the Lesson (5-10 minutes)

The Bible gives us signs to watch for, and something to wait for. Waiting is easier if you have something to do. And God gave us plenty to do while we wait! Pass out copies of the "Things to Do While We Wait" Activity Sheet.

After the students have had a chance to look up the Scriptures and write them down, go over them one at a time. **How can you practice self control? How can you live godly lives?** Some suggestions might include: continuing their Bible reading and prayer, being careful what they watch on television, and being careful about the way they talk.

How can you be witnesses? Who can you be a witness to? How can you be a witness to your friends and family by your actions? How can you witness with words?

Why might a Christian need encouraging? How can we encourage one another in this group?

Close in prayer, thanking God for His power, and asking Him to help us be strong so we will be ready for His return.

Sign of the Times

If **you were in charge** of putting up road signs that would let people know that the end of the age was near, *what would they say?*

© 1998 David C. Cook. Permission granted to reproduce for classroom use only.

 # A Few Things to Do While We Wait

Look up each of these Scriptures and write them down.
How can you put them into practice today?

Titus 2:11-13

2 Timothy 4:2

Acts 1:7

Hebrews 10:25

© 1998 David C. Cook. Permission granted to reproduce for classroom use only.

✔ Service Projects

1
Bibles on CD

The Bible is the most important thing a Christian can have. But there are people in almost every church who have to wait for someone else to read the Word of God to them. Is there an elderly person in your church who has trouble reading? Have your class collect cans or other recyclable items, hold a garage sale, have a bake sale, or organize some other fund-raiser to earn money for a CD player and the Bible on CD. Faith does come by hearing the Word of God—and so do comfort and courage! Have group members record a message to explain why they are giving the gift.

2
Encouragement Cards

The Bible tells us to encourage one another! Knowing that someone is praying for you can make it much easier to "take a stand." Talk with your pastor about someone in the community who is struggling. (It's better if he or she is not in your local church. That way he or she can't figure out who you are.) Have each student bring a greeting card to class. As a class, make a list of your favorite encouraging Scriptures. Write one Scripture on each card. Write something like:

Dear _____,
I will be praying for you on Saturday from _____ to _____.
Your friend, _____ (sign your first name only.)

Have each student choose a different day and time. (Make sure that your students understand that they have made a commitment to pray for this person during the hour they put on the card.) Mail the cards all at the same time.

3
Harvest Party

Hold a special Harvest Party celebrating the kind of harvest you can have at any time of year! Let everyone bring baked goods, chips, dip, and/or soda. Plan to show family movies. Before the date of the party, all students should think of the name of one person they know who doesn't go to church whom they can invite. As a class, commit to pray for your visitors before and after they attend your party. At the party, just make friends . . . but keep praying and reaching out to them. God wants them to be part of His great harvest!

© 1998 David C. Cook. Permission granted to reproduce for classroom use only.

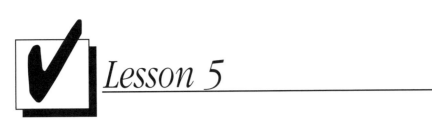

Notes

Making God's Values Our Values

We all learn values by living them. Trying to describe how you learned the values that you have now is not an easy task because your values are the result of a very gradual process that has involved everyone and everything around you since infancy.

Your students are at an important age—they are beginning to decide which values will be *their* values. The goal of this unit is to help your students see they can make *God's* values their values. But even biblical values cannot be *automatically* passed on. Children learn values by watching those around them, then patterning their own behavior after their role models. You now have the significant opportunity to be a part of that process. Over the next four weeks, you will teach four foundational Christian values—love for ourselves, love for others, integrity, and self-discipline. Your words will be influential, but remember that your actions and attitudes will do most of the teaching.

My Values Overview

Unit Verse: Put on the new self, created to be like God. Ephesians 4:24.
Unit Affirmation: I CAN MAKE GOD'S VALUES MY VALUES!

LESSON	TITLE	OBJECTIVE	SCRIPTURE BASE
Lesson #1	I Matter to God!	Students will understand how important they are to God and will decide to treat themselves as special and valued people.	Luke 15:8-10
Lesson #2	Other People Matter to God!	Students will understand how important other people are to God and will decide to treat others as special and valued people.	Luke 15:8-10
Lesson #3	I Will Live with Integrity!	Students will learn that integrity means doing the right thing even if no one else knows and will make action plans to apply the value of integrity to their lives.	Ephesians 4:21-32
Lesson #4	I Will Be Self-Disciplined!	Students will understand what it means to be self-disciplined and make action plans to apply the value of self-discipline to their lives.	Titus 2:11-14; 1 Timothy 4:7-8; Philippians 4:8
Also, see page 87 for a list of optional service projects for this unit.			

Partners

Students Make God's Values Their Own!

DEAR PARENTS: We hope this newsletter keeps you informed about and involved in what we're doing. After all, you *are your children's most important spiritual leaders. We want to be* your *partner any way we can.*

It happens to every parent.

Before you know it, you're not raising children anymore. You're raising young adults. They make decisions on their own. They think their own thoughts. They develop their own values.

Values are important to all of us. As Christians, although we want to pass along biblical values to our children, our values cannot automatically be passed on. However, when we understand where our values come from and how they are developed, it is easy for us to feel confident about our ability, with God's help, to share God's values so they can grow in our children's lives.

Values develop continually throughout our lifetimes but they are established most strongly during early and middle childhood. Upper elementary children pattern their lives after those around them. They watch those who care for them and take note of those things their parents care about.

As a result, your children are at an important age where they need to see you model biblical values. It is at this age that they become aware of any inconsistencies at home or at church. Their values may then be based on their conclusions as to why they may be hearing about one way to live but observing other ways. The significant factor in sharing your values with your children is living them consistently with and in front of your children.

Over the next few weeks, your "young adults" will be part of a group of students that will

Unit Verse:

Unit Verse: Put on the new self, created to be like God. Ephesians 4:24

Unit Affirmation:
I CAN MAKE GOD'S VALUES MY VALUES!

examine *their* values. We will look at four foundational Christian values. More important, we will teach your children that they can make God's values their values.

Principles

In this unit, your children will learn to make God's values their values. Review the following principles with your children.

PRINCIPLE #1
I MATTER TO GOD!

Your children are very important to God. The truth that God likes children in general and yours in particular is unchanging and wonderful. Since God sees value in your children, they can then value and respect themselves.

PRINCIPLE #2
OTHER PEOPLE MATTER TO GOD!

God's love and respect for people extends not just to your children but to all others as well. He values all persons regardless of their ability, age, or race and wants us to have that same attitude. Knowing that God respects and loves everyone will help your children do things to treat others with respect.

PRINCIPLE #3
I WILL LIVE WITH INTEGRITY!

Integrity is doing the right thing, even if no one else knows about it. God is our model for integrity. Integrity encompasses all the values that the Bible teaches us to live by, such as being honest, being consistent with our words and actions, and not using slander or malice. When your child puts the value of integrity into action, he or she is showing a personal commitment to live by God's values.

PRINCIPLE #4
I WILL BE SELF-DISCIPLINED!

Self-discipline can be defined as "making yourself do what you know you should, even when you don't feel like doing it." This takes practice and determination. Self-discipline is not always obvious to others but its effect on your children's lives is enormous. God's Word teaches us to say "NO" to the things in life that are not godly and "YES" to putting God's values into action.

pRaCtICe

1. Discuss your family's values.
As often as possible, talk together about the words and meanings of words that describe your family values. Call attention to examples you see in daily life, both of action that feflect your family's values and those that contradict them, and ask your children questions about what should or should not have happened. Since value development is a gradual, personal process, children need to reflect on all the options available to them in an open and accepting environment.

2. Make value jigsaw puzzles.
Use construction paper or large packing material (like styrofoam or cardboard) to make large, simple jigsaw puzzles of words that tell what our values are (like self-discipline, integrity, etc.) and their definitions. Decide together what words to use and what the definitions are. Use a marker to write the words on the surface, then cut in curving lines to create a puzzle. Make several different ones and use a timer or stop watch to see how quickly they can be assembled. After each puzzle is completed, alk about some examples of that value in action.

3. Let your children hear about and even participate in your own decisions and activities.
Since modeling is one of the most important ways to teach values, enhance your children's learning process by telling your family what choices you have made and why. For example, "I got a parking ticket today because I forgot to go back and put more money in the parking meter," or "I'm angry about the ticket, but it was fair, so I'll pay it as I should."

4. Volunteer as a family once a month at a local soup kitchen.
Before going, talk about ways to show the persons you will encounter that they are important to God and to you. Afterwards, find out if the children observed anyone being treated with disrespect and talk about what should have happened instead.

5. Ask "Why?" and "What if?" as often as possible and let your children do as much talking as possible.
Value development is enhanced by talking through issues to help your children clarify their own thinking. For example, talk about cheating on a test. Is cheating wrong if you don't get caught? Why or why not?

Unit Verse

Put on the new self,
created to be like God.
Ephesians 4:24.

I Can Make God's Values My Values!

I Matter to God!

Aim: Students will understand how important they are to God and will decide to treat themselves as special and valued people.

Scripture: Luke 15:8-10

Unit Verse: Put on the new self, created to be like God. Ephesians 4:24

Unit Affirmation: I CAN MAKE GOD'S VALUES MY VALUES!

1 Setting the Stage (5-10 minutes)

WHAT YOU'LL DO
- Make Friendship Bracelets.

WHAT YOU'LL NEED
- Yarn (3 colors, each cut into 12" strands)

2 Introducing the Issue (20 minutes)

WHAT YOU'LL DO
- Play "Valuegories" (brainstorm value categories) and discuss definitions of key terms.

WHAT YOU'LL NEED
- Paper, pencils, word cards, definition cards, WHAT IS IT? board, Unit Poster,
- OPTIONAL: Instant camera

PLANNING AHEAD
- Prepare the WHAT IS IT? Board by writing the heading "WHAT IS IT?" in large letters on posterboard (you will add to this display every week).
- Prepare the Word Cards by writing "Value" and "Actions" on index cards.
- Prepare the Definition Cards by writing definitions for "Value" and "Actions' (see Introducing the Issue) on index cards.
- Make the Unit Poster (see the directions on page 5 and poster on page 53).

3 Searching the Scriptures (20 minutes)

WHAT YOU'LL DO
- Pantomime the parable of the Lost Coin.

WHAT YOU'LL NEED
- Bibles, "The Lost Coin" Activity Sheet (page 60), name cards, props (including lamp, light, pennies or other coins), "Keeping My Values Safe" Activity Sheet (page 61)

PLANNING AHEAD
- Use 3" x 5" cards and 30" lengths of yarn to prepare name tags (see Searching the Scriptures)

4 Living the Lesson (5-10 minutes)

WHAT YOU'LL DO
- Complete a crossword puzzle about respect.

WHAT YOU'LL NEED
- "Respect for Myself" Activity Sheet (page 62), pencils

✔ Setting the Stage (5-10 minutes)

Have students make Friendship Bracelets. Ahead of time, prepare the yarn students need to make the bracelets: Using three different colors, cut one 12" length of yarn from each color for each student. Knot each group of three strands together at the end.

As students arrive today, give each one a small piece of tape and one of the knotted three-strand yarn lengths. Instruct them to tape the knotted end of the yarn to the edge of the table and braid the three strands together. While students are working, discuss: **Have you ever made friendship bracelets before? What are friendship bracelets used for?** If your students are not familiar with friendship bracelets, explain that they are often given as a gift to remind a friend that he or she is valued and important. While students are finishing the bracelets, encourage them to talk about some of their friendships. **Besides making friendship bracelets, how do you show your friends that they're important to you?** (Take responses.)

When a bracelet is braided, tie a knot in the untied end so it will not unravel. Have the students hold on to their bracelets until later in the lesson.

✔ Introducing the Issue (20 minutes)

Besides your friends, what are some things that are important to you? Discuss a wide range of possibilities, including both things students own and things students do. **If I had a chance to watch how you treat these important things, how could I tell they were important to you?**

What if you *said* something was important to you but you never did anything to show it? For example, what if you ignored your friend or said bad things about him or her? Can you really say your friend is important to you? (Probably not.) **What if we say something is important but then we do something completely different? What if you say you really like your dog but you kick it and hurt it?** Conclude this discussion by saying: **When something is really important to you, you show it by what you *do*.**

Play a game called "Valuegories," a variation of the popular party game Scattegories. Divide the students into teams of three or four and pass out paper and pens. For each round, read one of the items from the "important things list" on the next page. Give teams 20 seconds to write down at least five ways they could show that thing is important. For example, for the category "friends" teams might list: give a friendship bracelet, talk on the phone, spend time together, give compliments, or help a friend with homework problems. Any team that comes up with five or more legitimate answers gets

one point. Play as many rounds as you have time for. Here is the "important things list": Friend, Mom or Dad, pet dog, soccer team, school work, computer.

After the game, discuss: **People—like your mom or your best friend—can be important to you. Things—like your computer or your soccer ball—can be important to you. But there's one other type of thing that can be important to us, too. Any guesses?** (Pause for responses.) *Principles* **can also be important to us. Principles for living that are important to us are called values.** Ahead of time, write the word "Values" on its own index card. This is the Values Word Card. Also, write this definition on an index card: "Values are the principles that govern our lives." This is the Values Definition Card. Also, Give the Values Word Card and Definition Card to two different students to hold up. Have someone read the definition and talk about it together. **What are some examples of values?** (Being honest, obeying our parents, sharing.) **What does it mean when we say "values are the principles that govern our lives"?** (They help us make decisions and help us decide what's right and wrong.) Tape the Values Word Card and Definition Card on the WHAT IS IT? Board.

Play another few rounds of "Valuegories," this time using categories that include values like: honesty, sharing, unselfishness, and friendliness. For each value, require teams to produce three possible answers in 20 seconds. Encourage students to be as specific as they can when they come up with ideas for ways they can show the values in action. For example, for the category "honesty" students might list: Tell Mom you broke the vase; tell your teacher the real reason you didn't get your homework done; give back someone's wallet you found.

We're going to talk about VALUES for the next few weeks. The values we will talk about are God's values and He teaches us about them in the Bible. God's values are things that are important to God. As God's children and believers in His Son, Jesus, we want to live our lives as God wants us to live. We want God's values to be our values.

Display the Unit Poster. Repeat the Unit Affirmation together: I CAN MAKE GOD'S VALUES MY VALUES! Ask: *How* **can we make God's values our values? First, we have to find out what God's values are. How can we know what is valuable to God?** (Read the Bible, think about what God does, listen to your parents and Sunday school teacher.) **Once we know what God's values are, what can we do? We said that when something's important to us we show it by what we do and what we say. We show that God's values are our values by what we do and what we say, too. We can make the things that are important to God important to us.** Read the Unit Verse together. Explain the Unit Verse by saying: **We put on the new self by doing and saying things that God would want us to do.**

Lesson 1

✔ Searching the Scriptures (20 minutes)

Ahead of time, make name cards for the pantomime activity below. Punch holes in the upper corners of index cards. Tie a 30" length of yarn to each card, one end to each hole. Make one blank card for each student as well as three cards with the name "God" written on them and several extra blank cards.

What are some things that are important and valuable to God? What about you, yourself? Are you valuable? In what ways might you be valuable? To whom are you valuable? Take a few responses. **Most of us know we are important to our parents. What about to God? If you think you are important to God, how do you know that?**

Jesus often told stories to tell people what His values and God's values are. You will get the chance to participate in one of those stories. Watch and listen closely. Let's see if we can find any reasons to believe that we are important to God.

Distribute pencils, name cards, and copies of "The Lost Coin" Activity Sheet. Explain that volunteers will pantomime the scenes as directed on the Activity Sheet. (You may need to explain that a pantomime is action with no words or sounds.) Assign volunteers to the characters listed on the Activity Sheet. You can involve all your students who want a role by assigning as many Friends as needed. Have each actor write his or her character's name on any extra name cards.

When groups are ready, distribute Bibles and have students in the "audience" look up the Scripture passage listed on the Activity Sheet (Luke 15:8-10). Tell them they can refer to these verses to help answer the discussion questions you will ask after the pantomime.

Play the role of narrator. Begin reading Scene 1 off the Activity Sheet, pausing when necessary for students to complete their pantomime of the action. At the end of each scene actors should freeze in place, then the whole class (including the frozen actors) should discuss what happened.

After Scene 1, discuss: **What's wrong?** (The woman is missing a coin.) **Is the missing coin the only one the woman has?** (No.) **Is the coin that's lost any more valuable or worth more money than the ones that are left?** (No.) **Does it matter whether the coin is ever found? Why?**

After Scene 2, discuss: **What happened?** (The woman looked for the coin.) **Is the coin important to the woman? How do you know?** (She showed the coin is important to her by looking for it.)

After Scene 3, discuss: **Why is the woman so happy?** (She found something that was important to her.) **What did she do to show how she felt?** (She threw a party!)

At the end of the skit, discuss: **Jesus often told stories and parables that**

were like pictures. They often mean more than you might think the first time you hear the story. Did anyone see the message in this story? Supplement students' answers by saying: **Some of the things in the story represent something else. In this story of the Lost Coin, the woman represents God.** Give the extra name card labeled "God" to the student playing the woman. **Who does the lost coin represent?** (You or me.) Have the person playing the role of the Coin flip his or her name card over and write his or her own name on the card.

Have the actors perform the skit again, from start to finish without any narration or pauses. Actors can refer to their copies of the Activity Sheet to know what to do next.

Discuss: **What was God missing?** (Name of the actor who the played the Coin.) **Did it matter to God that the person was missing? Was the person in the skit any more valuable than any other person in the world?** (No.) **So if God went to look for (actor's name), would He go and look for you too if you were lost? Would he throw a party if He found you?** (Yes.)

Before God found us, how were we lost? (We didn't have a relationship with God.) **How did God go to look for us?** (He sent His Son, Jesus, to tell us how to have a relationship with Him and then to die for our sins so we could have a relationship with Him.) **Those are some pretty amazing ways God showed us that we're important to Him, aren't they?**

We said that values are the principles that are important to us. What "principle" was important to God? What *value* **did God show when He sent His Son to find us and save us?** There may be a number of good answers but make sure to mention this one: **One of God's highest values is love, specifically love for each one of us. His love for us is so important that He showed it by sending His Son to earth to die for our sins.**

Refer back to the Friendship Bracelets students made at the beginning of the lesson. Tell them to help one another tie the bracelets on their wrists. Tell students when they look at these bracelets to remember God's love for them.

We said that we want God's values to be our values. If one of God's highest values is love for us, how can we make that one of our values? (We can value ourselves as highly as God does.) Explain that loving ourselves doesn't mean being selfish or thinking of ourselves as more important than others. It does mean that we can feel good about ourselves because of God's love for us.

Distribute copies of the "Keeping My Values Safe" Activity Sheet (page 61). **What is one way you can guard an object that is very valuable?** (If no one mentions "Put it in a safe," mention it yourself.) **Our values need to be guarded and protected. We guard them by doing things to show they are important to us, instead of doing things that are the opposite of our values.**

Help students assemble their "value safes" as follows: Cut off the heading from the top of the page and the copyright information from the bottom of the page. The resource now contains three sections: a picture of the right side of the safe, one of the back of the safe, and one of the left side of the safe. Make two folds, one between the right side and back side of the safe, and one between the left side and back side of the safe. The safe now opens up as if with double doors.

Have students draw lines to divide the inside of the safe into four sections. **We'll use one section for each lesson. Today, use the first section and write the words "I matter to God—God loves me!" near the top. Then write or draw something to show what action you will do since this is one of your values.** When students are done, collect and keep the safes for use in coming weeks. (In other lessons, these will be referred to as "Values Safes.")

✔ Living the Lesson (5-10 minutes)

God values you and His actions show He loves you. Even if you aren't interested in knowing God, He still loves you. He will always want you to know Him and love Him back.

Talk about wearing the Friendship Bracelet to help remember that you are valued by God. **Since God thinks I'm valuable, I'll remember to treat my body, mind, and spirit with respect also. What are some ways we can treat ourselves with respect?** Distribute copies of the "Respect for Myself" Activity Sheet (page 62) and have the students work together to complete it.

Close the class by asking volunteers to complete this sentence. "I'm thankful that I am valuable to God because . . . ." Then pray together a prayer of thanks that we can value ourselves since we know that God values us.

 **The Lost Coin**

Luke 15:8-10

3 or more characters: *Woman, Coin, Friend(s)*

SCENE 1: The woman reaches into her pocket and smiles as she pulls out a few coins. She counts them and then frowns. She counts them again, and then starts looking all around her.

SCENE 2: *(The student who is the coin should be hiding in the room.)* The woman lights a lamp and sweeps her whole house. She looks carefully under everything. She can't find the coin. She frowns.

SCENE 3: After searching for the coin for a long time, she finally finds it and looks very happy. The woman goes outside the house and calls to her neighbors and friends to come inside and share her happiness. They sit down on the floor together and clap and sing.

© 1998 David C. Cook. Permission granted to reproduce for classroom use only.

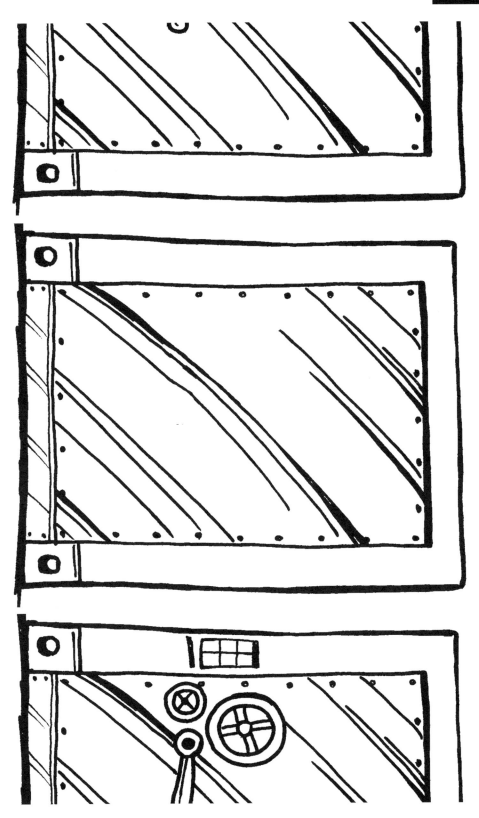

© 1998 David C. Cook. Permission granted to reproduce for classroom use only.

✔ Respect for Myself

1. Read the statements below. They will remind you of ways you can show respect for yourself.
2. Find the underlined words in the word find.

Extra: There are three other words in the word find that aren't listed! Put these three words in the blanks at the bottom of the page to find out what God thinks about you.

Just as God treats me with respect,
I treat myself with respect when I take care of my . . .

Body: *Get lots of* <u>exercise</u>, *plenty of* <u>sleep</u>, *and eat* <u>nutritious</u> *food*

Mind: *Do my best in* <u>school</u>, <u>read</u> *my Bible, and think about what is* <u>pure</u> *and right.*

Spirit: *Thank* <u>Jesus</u> *for* <u>loving</u> *me,* <u>pray</u> *every day, and* <u>worship</u> *God in church.*

```
L   E   G   O   D   S   L   E   E   P
O   X   Q   W   V   C   M   Y   L   P
V   E   M   Z   R   H   M   O   F   W
I   R   L   E   B   O   I   P   M   O
N   C   D   O   C   O   N   R   E   R
G   I   P   F   V   L   D   A   N   S
R   S   P   U   R   E   G   Y   D   H
R   E   A   D   J   E   S   U   S   I
P   Z   Y   S   P   I   R   I   T   P
N   U   T   R   I   T   I   O   U   S
```

G ___ ___   L ___ ___ ___ ___   M ___ .

© 1998 David C. Cook. Permission granted to reproduce for classroom use only.

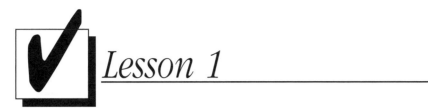

Notes

Other People Matter to God!

Aim: Students will understand how important other people are to God and will decide to treat others as special and valued people.

Scripture: Luke 15:8-10

Unit Verse: Put on the new self, created to be like God. Ephesians 4:24

Unit Affirmation: I CAN MAKE GOD'S VALUES MY VALUES!

1 Setting the Stage (5-10 minutes)

WHAT YOU'LL DO
- Make a collage of faces.

WHAT YOU'LL NEED
- Old magazines and newspapers, scissors, tape, paper, WHAT IS IT? board from Lesson 1

PLANNING AHEAD
- Use old magazines and newspapers and cut out pictures of people of all ages, races, economic status, physical abilities, professions and disabilities.
- Cut 5" x 8 ½" pieces of construction paper or card stock for the collage background, one for each student.

2 Introducing the Issue (20 minutes)

WHAT YOU'LL DO
- Complete an activity sheet about valuing others.

WHAT YOU'LL NEED
- "Other People Matter" Activity Sheet (page 69), pencils, candy, Unit Poster

3 Searching the Scriptures (20 minutes)

WHAT YOU'LL DO
- Pantomime the parable of the Lost Coin.

WHAT YOU'LL NEED
- Bibles, "The Lost Coin" Activity Sheet (page 60), name tags, props
- Values Safes from Lesson 1

PLANNING AHEAD
- Use 3" x 5" cards and a 30" length of yarn to make name tags as described in Searching the Scriptures.

4 Living the Lesson (5-10 minutes)

WHAT YOU'LL DO
- Write letters to show respect to others.

WHAT YOU'LL NEED
- "Do Something to Show Others Matter" Activity Sheet (page 70); pencils, colored markers, and/or crayons

Lesson 2

✔ Setting the Stage (5-10 minutes)

As your students arrive today, have them use the magazine pictures you've collected ahead of time to make collages of faces or people that will be used as a border for the WHAT IS IT? Board. Distribute collage supplies (scissors, glue, and the strips of construction paper you've already cut into pieces that will fit as a border around the WHAT IS IT? BOARD). Explain that in a collage the pictures should cover the entire paper without leaving any spaces between them. As needed, assist students in finding pictures of people that show as much variety as possible, including people who are smiling, frowning, sad, mad, tall, short, all ages, all races, all abilities, etc.

When the collages are finished, tape or staple them around the outside edge of the bulletin board to form a border. Gather the students together and talk about the pictures as you look at them together. **Who are the people in these pictures? Who knows them?** (Their families and friends, God.) **Do you think God knows each one of these people? Which of these people do you think are more valuable to God? Why? Do you think God likes the ones who are smiling more than the sad ones? Do you think God knows more about you than He does about some of these other people? Why or why not?**

✔ Introducing the Issue (20 minutes)

Last week we talked about something so valuable that we were going to protect it all of our lives. Some of you are still wearing your friendship bracelets to help you remember. What was it we were trying to remember? (I matter to God.)

God wants us to have the same attitude that He does. God knows and does what is right and He wants us to do that also. If every other person in the world is important to God and God likes each one just the same—no matter who they are or what they do—how does God want us to treat other people?

Use a simple, arbitrary way to divide the students into several groups. For example, you might divide them by a color they are wearing, or the types of shoes they have on, or what they ate for breakfast.

Ask those who are wearing something blue (for example) to stand against the left wall, those with red on to stand at the back of the room, and those with neither red nor blue to stand near the door.

If you are wearing red today, are you more important to God than those who are not wearing red? (No.) **Are you different from those who are not wearing red?** (Yes, the colors in your clothes are different.) **Can all of you be**

different and all just as important to God at the same time? We are all very different in many ways. But each of us is just as valuable to God as anyone else. What are some ways you are all different? What are ways you are all the same?

My favorite color is blue, so will all of you wearing blue come and sit close to me. The rest of you can stand in the back of the room. To further illustrate this random favoritism, pass out a piece of candy to each of the students wearing blue. Discuss: Was I showing those who have blue on that they are more valuable to me? Are they really more valuable? Is this how God wants us to treat other people—as if some are more important than others? Are you blue people more important than others in the world? No one in the world is more important than any other person in the world, not even the most famous person in the world. Ask for some suggestions of famous people.

Does God think that (a famous person) is more important than you? Are adults more important than children? than babies? No, every person matters to God just the same. Sometimes this is hard to remember because a lot of people think that they are more important than others. Sometimes people look at others who are different in some way and think, "They're not important at all!" But this is not how God thinks, and God wants us to think the way He does.

What does God do to show that people matter to Him? (Review from Lesson 1: He sent His Son to find us when we were lost and to die for our sins.) What can we do to show that other people matter to us? Distribute copies of the "Other People Matter" Activity Sheet (page 69) and have students complete it. Discuss some of the things they have circled or added to the page.

Today, we are talking about how much God values other people and how important they are to Him. Knowing that they are important to God will help us remember that they should be important to us. God treats people with respect and value and so should we. Display the Unit Poster, and have the class read the Unit Affirmation aloud together.

Lesson 2

✔ Searching the Scriptures (20 minutes)

Jesus told some stories in the Bible that tell us how important all people are to God. See if you recognize this story.

Use yarn and index cards to make more name cards the same way you did for Lesson 1. Leave most of the name cards blank but label some of them with things like: "Homeless with ragged clothes"; "Someone who is mean to you"; "Child from another country who doesn't speak your language well."

Do you remember the Bible story from last week? Something was lost. What was it? What did the lost thing represent? Who was looking for the coin? Who did she represent? Review that the lost coin represented each of us and the woman represented God.

Today, we're going to talk about the same story, but there will be some small differences. See if you can notice what they are.

Distribute copies of "The Lost Coin" Activity Sheet from Lesson 1 (page 60). Give instructions similar to Lesson 1: Assign volunteers to the characters listed on the activity sheet and play the part of the narrator yourself. Give each actor a name card to wear. Tell the person playing the part of the Woman to wear the name card that says "God" again. Have the student playing the part of the coin wear the name card of "Homeless with ragged clothes."

Let the student playing the role of the Woman know that she will do something different in Scenes 2 and 3 than she did in Lesson 1. Start the skit.

After Scene 1, discuss: **Have you noticed anything different yet about this story?** (Probably not.)

Now, narrate this modification of Scene 2: *(The student who is the coin should be hiding in the room.)* The woman briefly looks around but does not see the coin. She shrugs her shoulders and doesn't really care.

After Scene 2, discuss: **Have you noticed anything different yet? What? According to this skit, is the missing person important to God? How do you know? Do you think this is how God really would act? Why or why not?**

Finish the modified skit by reading this new narration for Scene 3: Since the Woman didn't really care about the coin, she didn't look for it. Then she thought that she was starting to get hungry, so she started to prepare dinner and forgot about the coin.

After Scene 3, discuss: **How do you think the lost person feels? It looks like no one cares about this person. What does the name card say?** (Read the students' name card.) **Is this the way Jesus told this story? Could this really happen—would God ever act like He didn't care about somebody because that person looked different or didn't have a home? Why?**

Of course we know that God would not act like someone didn't matter. The story in the Bible tells us for certain that God treats everyone the same. God loves everyone. That means that other people are valuable to God. People—all kinds of people—are valuable to God. As God's children, we want God's values to become our values. **What can we do to show that others also matter to us?**

Distribute the Values Safes you collected at the end of Lesson 1. Have students write the words "Other people matter to God and to me" in the second section. Then have them draw or write something in the space beside it to show what they will do to show that another person is important to them. When students are finished, collect the safes again.

✔ Living the Lesson (5-10 minutes)

We know that God values each person in the world. So how should we treat other people? Ask for volunteers to tell about some of the things they wrote or drew about on their "Values Safes."

Sometimes it is easy to show our family and friends that they matter to us, but what about people you don't know? Does God treat people from other countries differently from the way He treats you? Can you think of some ways to show people you don't know that they matter to God and to you?

Talk about some of the things that are being done locally to help people in need, such as a shelter for the homeless or soup kitchen for the hungry. Ask the students for suggestions of things they might do to help people they don't know, such as save their allowances, collect used clothing, or distribute canned food. **What are some specific ways you can show others you respect and value them?**

Distribute copies of the "Do Something to Show Others Matter" Activity Sheet, pencils, and/or colored markers or crayons. Instruct students to write a letter to someone. Their letter can be to someone they know to tell them how valuable they are and how much they matter. Or they may choose to write a letter to the editor of the newspaper, to a local politician, or to businesses to ask that something be done to help people who need it. Other students may want to write a letter to the newspaper to explain what they as students can do to show their respect for other people. Some possibilities might include visiting a retirement center or collecting outdated food from grocery stores and restaurants for homeless shelters. Tell the students that you will mail their completed letters and let them know when you get an answer.

Close the lesson by praying that God will help you show others that they matter.

Other People Matter ✔

Circle the words that show what you can do to show people you respect them.

I can show other people matter to me by **WORDS** *that are . . .*

RUDE	*Caring*	KIND
Name calling	**Angry**	Thoughtful
Put down	_____	**Cheerful**
	(Fill in)	

I can show other people matter to me by **ACTIONS** *when I . . .*

Help	SMILE	Share
Ignore	**Yell**	_____
		(Fill in)
Mean	PRAY	

Who is valuable to me?

I will *show* **respect** to **others** *this week* by:

© 1998 David C. Cook. Permission granted to reproduce for classroom use only.

✔ Do Something to Show Others Matter

Write a letter to show you have respect for others.
Design a border around the outside edge of your letter.

Date _____

Dear _____,

I have been learning about God's values. One of God's values is other people matter to Him just like I do! I want God's values to be my values and I want to show my respect to others just as God does.

One way I want to show my respect is to

Please remember that God loves every person. He thinks you are very important, and I agree!

Love, _____

Decorate this label to use when you send your letter.

_____
_____
_____

© 1998 David C. Cook. Permission granted to reproduce for classroom use only.

Lesson 2

Notes

My Values

I Will Live With Integrity!

Aim: Students will learn that integrity means doing the right thing even if no one else knows and will make action plans to apply the value of integrity to their lives.

Scripture: Ephesians 4:21-32

Unit Verse: Put on the new self, created to be like God. Ephesians 4:24

Unit Affirmation: I CAN MAKE GOD'S VALUES MY VALUES!

1 Setting the Stage (5-10 minutes)

WHAT YOU'LL DO
- Practice stacking paper cups.

WHAT YOU'LL NEED
- Paper cups

2 Introducing the Issue (20 minutes)

WHAT YOU'LL DO
- Discuss case studies about integrity.

WHAT YOU'LL NEED
- Paper cups from Setting the Stage, markers, "What Will They Do?" Activity Sheet (page 77), chalkboard
- Unit Poster
- WHAT IS IT? Board from Lesson 1, Word Card and Definition Card for "Integrity"

PLANNING AHEAD
- Make a Word Card and a Definition Card for "integrity" (see Introducing the Issue).

3 Searching the Scriptures (20 minutes)

WHAT YOU'LL DO
- Complete an activity sheet about what the Bible says about integrity.

WHAT YOU'LL NEED
- Bibles, "Words About Integrity" Activity Sheet (page 78), Values Safes from Lesson 2

4 Living the Lesson (5-10 minutes)

WHAT YOU'LL DO
- Write prayers to God on paper cups.

WHAT YOU'LL NEED
- Paper Cups from Introducing the Issue

✔ Setting the Stage (5-10 minutes)

As your students arrive, give each person about 20 three-ounce paper cups. Tell each student to find a place in the room away from others and see how many cups he or she can stack on top of each other. (The cups are to be stacked open end to open end and base end to base end, with every other cup upside down.) Students can start over as many times as necessary until you call time. They should keep track of the highest number of cups they stack before their tower of cups falls. However, they should NOT tell anyone else how many cups they were able to stack.

Was this a difficult game? What was the hardest thing about it? Don't tell anyone how many cups you had in your highest stack, but keep track of that number in your head. Ask those who stacked more than 15 cups in one stack to go stand in one particular area of the room. Ask those who stacked between 7 and 15 to stand in a different area, and those with fewer than 7 cups to stand in a third area. **In one sense, it doesn't really matter where you're standing right now. There are no "winners" in this game. All I said was for everyone to stack as many cups as you could and you all did as many as you could. But in another sense, it does matter a lot where you're standing. It matters because it shows how honest you are when no one else knows. No one else knows how many cups were in your largest stack. No one else knows where you should be standing. Only you know if you have been honest. We're going to talk today about doing what's right, even when no one else knows.**

✔ Introducing the Issue (20 minutes)

Have each student keep nine paper cups and use a marker to write the letters I-N-T-E-G-R-I-T-Y on the bottoms of the cups, one letter per cup. **Do you know what this word is? What does it mean? In the game we just played, when you were honest about following the instructions of the game, even when no one else knew about it, you were showing you have the value of "integrity."** Ahead of time, write this definition of "integrity" on a definition card: "Integrity is doing what you know is right, even when no one else is looking." Also, write the word "Integrity" on its own Word Card. have someone put up the word card INTEGRITY and its definition on the WHAT IS IT? Board.

Integrity involves what you do, what you say, and even what you think. When you practice integrity, you try to do the right thing, no matter what. If "doing the right thing, even if no one knows" is one way to describe integrity, what would be the opposite of integrity?

Since integrity is such an important and involved thing, let's spend a few minutes thinking about what it is and also what it is not. Distribute copies of the "What Will They Do?" Activity Sheet. The two scenarios on the top of this sheet require students to decide whether or not the characters will practice integrity. Read the scenarios one at a time and ask for pairs of volunteers to roleplay a possible ending. Every student should follow the directions on the sheet and draw or write their own ideas for possible responses. Discuss: **What would be the right thing to do in this situation? What would be some examples of some wrong things to do in this situation?** Let volunteers share what they wrote or drew on their activity sheets.

> OPTIONAL: If time allows, have students roleplay some wrong ways to respond to the three scenarios on the bottom of the activity sheet. Have other groups roleplay some right ways to respond.

Having integrity isn't just one thing. It's many things. It's a *lifestyle*. What are some words that describe what you would do when you have integrity? Write INTEGRITY on the chalkboard and list the words students provide (care, love, be honest, and so on). **What are some words that describe what you would not do when you have integrity?** Write NO INTEGRITY on the chalkboard and list the words the students provide (lie, steal, cheat, and so on).

We said that integrity is doing the right thing, even if no one else knows. But there are always two people who know. Who are they? (You and God.) **Why does that matter?** (As Christians, we know that God wants us to do the right thing.) Display the Unit Poster and have the class read the Unit Affirmation statement aloud together. **The Bible teaches us who God is, what He is like, and what His values are. As we learn more and more about God and His Son, Jesus, we are learning about God's standards for how we are to live our lives. Today we will see what the Bible teaches about the value of integrity.** Read the Unit Verse. Have the students repeat the Unit Verse back to you.

 # Searching the Scriptures (20 minutes)

There is a symbol that is used everywhere in the world to show you what to do or not to do even if you can't read the language of the country you are in. Where have you seen signs that look like this? Draw on the chalkboard the international symbol of a circle with a line diagonally across it. **What do you do when you see a sign like this?** (If there is no line across the circle, you do what it says; if there is a line across it, you do not do it.) Draw a circle with a hand inside, then draw a line across to show you should not touch. Ask students for other examples and draw them to illustrate. **What might happen if you don't obey these signs?**

Today's Scripture explains some things we are to do and not to do. Listen for words and actions that should be in a circle with a line across it. When you hear one, hold up your forearm across your face, so it will look like there is a line across it. Also listen for words and actions that should be in a circle without the line across it. These are things we should do. When you hear one, make a circle with your thumb and forefinger (the international sign for okay). As you read today's scripture, Ephesians 4:21-32, pause after the words the students should respond to.

Did you understand what all the words in this verse mean? What does falsehood mean? slander? malice?

Distribute Bibles and copies of the "Words about Integrity" Activity Sheet. Ask for a volunteer to read the directions and then assist students in completing the sheet.

Review the circles that students put a line through. They should be: falsehood, slander, unwholesome talk, stealing, and malice. Compare these to the list of NO INTEGRITY words you made in Introducing the Issue. Add any words from the activity sheet that are not already on the list. Review the words that students did not put a line through. They should include: kind, forgiving, talk that is helpful, compassion, and speak truthfully. Compare these to the list of INTEGRITY words on the board and add any words that are not already on the list.

When something matters to God, it should matter to us. Integrity matters to God so it should matter to us. Doing everything with integrity is so important, we need to guard it. We keep it safe by our actions. When we keep doing things that are the opposite of integrity, we can lose this value—we show that it isn't important to us and we don't care whether we have it or not. Integrity belongs in our safe as God's value and one of our values. Distribute the Values Safes from Lesson 2 and have students write "I will do what is right because it matters to God" in the third section. Have them write or draw something in the space beside it to show an action they will use to put the value in action. When students are done, collect the Values Safes one more time.

✔ Living the Lesson (5-10 minutes)

Direct students' attention to the paper cups that they should still have marked I-N-T-E-G-R-I-T-Y. Pass out pens. Tell students to think about the areas in their life that are hardest for them to have integrity. Tell them to take the cup marked "I" and complete the sentence, "I have a hard time with integrity when . . ." on the inside of that cup. Tell them to take the cup marked "N" and complete the sentence, "In order to have integrity, I will say

No to . . ." on the inside of that cup. Finally, tell them to take the cup marked "G" and complete the sentence, "Dear God, I want to have integrity. Please help me to . . ." on the inside of that cup.

Close the lesson by having the students pray together to ask God to help them live with integrity. Have them take home the cups with the letters of INTEGRITY written on them to remind them how important integrity is to God and to each of us.

What Will They Do? ✔

JANIE IS TALKING ON THE PHONE:	You want me to come to your party on Saturday, Myra? Sure, I'll be there! *(Hangs up phone.)*
Darlene is nearby and heard what Janie said on the phone.	
DARLENE SAYS TO JANIE:	Are you kidding? I'd never go to HER party. It'd be a waste.
JANIE:	Now what do I do? I don't want to go if you think it'd be awful.
DARLENE:	Just don't go. It's not like you promised her you'd be there. Is it?
JANIE:	Well, yes, it is like a promise.

On the back of this sheet, write or draw what Janie should do about the party.

Did you show that Janie has integrity?   YES   NO

Tim sees Joe across the street and calls:	Hey, Joe, finish the homework?
Joe:	Yeah, it wasn't too bad. What about you?
Tim:	I didn't have time! But if you let me borrow yours, I'll give you five bucks. What do you think? It's like free money; you've already done the work!"

On the back of this sheet, write or draw what Joe should do.

Did you show that Joe has integrity?   YES   NO

What about this?

1. You use bad language when you are with your friends but are very careful with your words around your family. What could you do instead?

2. You complain about your teacher to your parents but tell your teacher how much you like the things he does. What could you do instead?

3. You tell your sister to say you aren't home when your friend telephones, even though you are in the other room listening to music. What could you do instead?

© 1998 David C. Cook. Permission granted to reproduce for classroom use only.

Words about Integrity

PART 1: To Do or Not To Do

Read Ephesians 4:21-32 in your Bible. Write the number of the Bible verse under any words you find in your Bible. Make the symbol for DO NOT by putting a diagonal line across the circle if someone with integrity WOULD NOT do it.

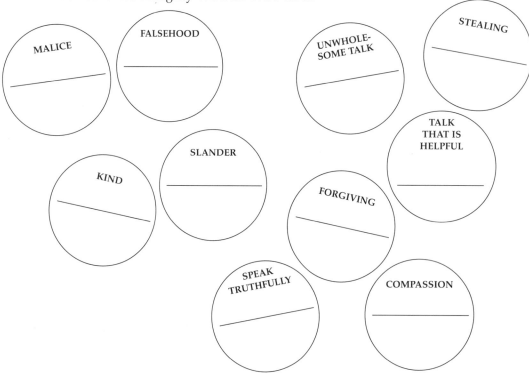

Draw lines to match the words and definitions from Ephesians 4:21-32.

PART 2: But What Does It Mean?

1. **Integrity**   A. Something said to try to deceive, a lie

2. **Slander**   B. Wanting to hurt someone on purpose

3. **Malice**   C. Doing the right thing (even when no one knows)

4. **Falsehood**   D. Taking something that isn't yours

5. **Speak truthfully**   E. Saying an untrue thing that damages another person's reputation

6. **Unwholesome   F. Letting go of your anger and stop blaming the one
   talk**   who hurt you

7. **Stealing**   G. Being honest with your words

8. **Compassion**   H. Having concern for another person and doing something to help

9. **Forgiving**   I. Talk that is mean, impure, or not helpful to others

1 - C, 2 - E, 3 - B, 4 - A, 5 - G, 6 - I, 7 - D, 8 - H, 9 - F.

© 1998 David C. Cook. Permission granted to reproduce for classroom use only.

Notes

My Values

I Will Be Self-disciplined!

Aim: Students will understand what it means to be self-disciplined and make action plans to apply the value of self-discipline to their lives.

Scripture: Titus 2:11-14; 1 Timothy 4:7-8; and Philippians 4:8

Unit Verse: Put on the new self, created to be like God. Ephesians 4:24

Unit Affirmation: I CAN MAKE GOD'S VALUES MY VALUES!

1 Setting the Stage (5-10 minutes)

WHAT YOU'LL DO
- Practice throwing paper into a wastebasket.

WHAT YOU'LL NEED
- Paper wads, wastebaskets

2 Introducing the Issue (20 minutes)

WHAT YOU'LL DO
- Complete an activity sheet about self-discipline.

WHAT YOU'LL NEED
- Word card and definition card for SELF-DISCIPLINE, WHAT IS IT? board, copies of "Time to Use Self-Discipline" Activity Sheet (page 85)
- Unit Poster

PLANNING AHEAD
- Prepare Word and Definition Cards for "Self-Discipline" (see Introducing the Issue).

3 Searching the Scriptures (20 minutes)

WHAT YOU'LL DO
- Study what the Bible says about self-discipline and use a chart to reinforce the lesson.

WHAT YOU'LL NEED
- Bibles, chalkboard and chalk or a large sheet of paper and marker, Unit Safes from Lesson 3

4 Living the Lesson (5-10 minutes)

WHAT YOU'LL DO
- Complete an activity sheet about choosing actions.

WHAT YOU'LL NEED
- Copies of "Choosing My Actions" Activity Sheet (page 86)

Lesson 4

✔ Setting the Stage (5-10 minutes)

Set several wastebaskets around the room. When students enter, give each 10-15 pieces of scratch paper. Tell students to wad up their papers and practice tossing them into one of the wastebaskets from 5-10 feet away. When they have used up all their paper wads, they should regather all the wads from the floor or the wastebasket and start over.

Did any of you feel like your aim was getting better the more you practiced tossing the paper into the basket? What if you had hours and hours or even days and days to practice—do you think your aim would get better with all that practice?

You may not know it, but you were already putting into practice the value we're going to talk about today. Let me describe the value and you see if you can guess what it is. This value is something that almost everyone uses sometimes, but almost no one uses enough. It is something that everyone must have, but not everyone thinks it's important. You can have a better time with your family and your friends when you have this value. You can become an excellent swimmer or a violinist with this value. Any guesses?

✔ Introducing the Issue (20 minutes)

The first part of the name of today's value is SELF. What is that? (You, yourself.) **The second part of the name of this value is DISCIPLINE. What does that mean?** (Training, practice doing right.)

What is different about discipline when you put the word "self" in front of it? (You are the one who does the disciplining. You discipline yourself.) Ahead of time, make a word and definition card for self-discipline. On the Definition Card write, "Self-discipline is making yourself do what you know you should do, even when you don't feel like doing it." Have volunteers put the Word Card and Definition Card on the WHAT IS IT? Board.

Can you make yourself do the things you should? What are some things you might not want to do but you know you are supposed to? (Help around the house, pick up clothes, do homework, speak kindly to brothers and sisters, practice the piano.) **Those things might not sound very hard to do, but what makes them so difficult? This sounds like the term, "self-discipline." Self-discipline is knowing you *can* do it, but sometimes making yourself do it because you would rather not.**

Have a conversation with yourself. Pretend there is a computer or a TV in front of you and you are sitting on the floor watching something or playing a computer game. Make sure students actually do this; they should turn to sit as if watching something. **Then all of a sudden you remember that you told your Mom you would set the table and peel the potatoes**

before five o'clock! **You even told her not to remind you. You look at the clock. It's 4:50! So what do you do?** Ask several students to describe the conversation they might have with themselves, inside their heads.

Which students used self-discipline when they told themselves what to do? What kind of consequences do you think you might have received if you did not use self-discipline? How would self-discipline have helped you do both things—watch the TV or play your game and get your chores done on time? (If you had self-discipline, you could have MADE yourself get up and do what you needed to do before anything else.)

Self-discipline is not always just doing things you don't want to do. Sometimes self-discipline is needed to help you keep doing things you like and you want to get better at. If you want to be a better ballplayer or a better writer or a better piano player, you use self-discipline to make yourself practice. When you make yourself practice even when you don't want to, that's using self-discipline. What are some things you might need to practice so you could be really good at doing it? Pause for responses.

Pass out copies of the "Time for Self-discipline" Activity Sheet. **What are some other ways you can benefit from practice besides tossing paper wads into a wastebasket? Think about something you might like to do when you are an adult. Would you need to practice a lot before you could get a job? That practice will take self-discipline. Maybe you are thinking of something you can start practicing now. Make a note of it on the activity sheet.**

Display the Unit Poster and have the class read the Unit Affirmation together. Read the Unit Verse together. **God always does the right thing. And when God's Son, Jesus, was on earth there were times when it might have been easier for Him not to do the right thing. But He always had self-discipline. We know that self-discipline is one of God's values because we see it in Jesus' life. If self-discipline was one of God's values, it can be one of our values, too.**

✔ Searching the Scriptures (20 minutes)

Ahead of time, list the following questions on the chalkboard or posterboard:

What to do?
Who?
When?
Where?
Why?

Lesson 4

And:

In the Bible

Titus 2:11-14	Say _____ to ungodliness/wrong things.
	Live _____ lives.
Philippians 4:8	_____ about such things.
1 Timothy 4:7-8	_____ yourself to be _____.

Distribute Bibles and bookmarks to the students and assist them in finding the three Bible passages listed on the chalkboard. Have them put a bookmark at each place so it can be easily found at the right time in the discussion.

The Bible tells us some things we are to do and not do as we practice self-discipline. As we read, first we need to find the words that tell us what to do. We'll use these words to complete the puzzle on the chalkboard. Then we'll fill in the rest of the questions.

Read Titus 2:11-14 aloud. Have students follow along in their own Bibles. **Did you find some words we should write in the puzzle?** Write "no" and "self-controlled" on the first two lines. **What's another way to say "self-controlled?"** (Self-disciplined.) **How does being self-disciplined help us live the way God wants us to?** (We can say no to the things God wants us to.) **What does ungodliness means?** (Not godly, not living like God wants us to.)

Have students find their bookmark for Philippians 4:8. Have someone read these verses. **Did you find any words that belong on the puzzle?** Write "think" on the appropriate line of the puzzle. **What are some things that are good to think about? What are some things that we shouldn't think about?** Take several examples. **In what ways should you practice self-discipline to help you think about the right things?**

Finish the puzzle by having the students find and read 1 Timothy 4:7-8. Write "Train" and "godly" in the last lines of the puzzle. Talk about training as practicing to use our minds or our bodies, such as exercise. **What are some things you can do to train yourself so that you will do what God wants you to do?**

What about the rest of the puzzle? WHO should do these things? Do you remember what the Bible said? Write something like "us" or "yourself" next to the line that says, "Who?" **Can your parents be self-disciplined for you? Can you just let your friends think about the right things for you?**

WHEN do you think we should do these things? Does the Bible say a specific time? (No). **What do you think we should write in here?** (Write something like, "All the time.")

Divide the students into groups of about four or five for the next two questions. Distribute paper and pencils, then give them the following directions: **These Bible verses don't say exactly where or why we are to do**

these things, but I know you can figure it out. First, in your group, think of at least three reasons WHY you think we are to do the things listed here. Then make a list of five places WHERE you go when you should practice self-discipline. This list must be a list of real places where you would need to use self-discipline. But for fun, try to be as creative as you can. Try to come up with some ideas that no other group can.

Give the groups a few minutes to write down their ideas, then ask them for their answers. Finally ask them WHY and write some of their responses on the board.

What are some places you have written down for WHERE you need to use self-discipline? Write down the places they name for using self-discipline every day. See which group came up with the most unique places that aren't on any other group's list.

Distribute the Values Safes that students have worked on in the first three lessons. Self-discipline is such an important value that it must be kept safe by practicing it everyday. Write "self-discipline" on the last section inside your safes, then draw or write one thing you can do to use your self-discipline. Discuss some possibilities for actions that will use self-discipline and allow time for the students to write or draw. Send the safes home with the students.

✔ Living the Lesson (5-10 minutes)

When we think about how God wants us to live, we need to think about the things we do every day. What are the values that we have been talking about? (I matter to God, other people matter to God, I will live with integrity, and I will live with self-discipline.)

Distribute the "Choosing My Actions" Activity Sheet (page 86). God knows the things that are hard for you to do and He wants to help you be self-disciplined. Read the directions for the activity sheet together and allow time for the students to complete this.

It isn't always easy to be self-disciplined. Even adults have a hard time and need to keep practicing self-discipline. However, we have someone who wants to help us live this value. Since this is also God's value, God wants you to ask Him for help when it is hard for you to use self-discipline. The good thing about prayer is that you can pray as fast as you can think, so when you know you should do something and are trying to decide what to do, think a prayer right then. What words could you say in your mind? Have the students suggest some brief prayers that could be used to ask God for His help "on the spot."

Close the unit with thanks to God that He is helping us learn to live by His values.

Time for Self-Discipline

Practice what you like to do! Even something fun takes self-discipline when you have to practice a lot.

What is something you are practicing so you'll do it better?

Sport _____

Musical instrument _____

Writing _____

Cooking _____

Other _____

Other _____

Draw pictures of what you do on the clock near the time that you practice.

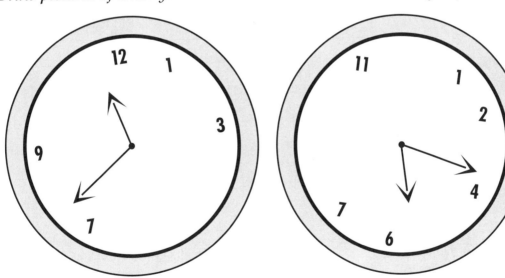

This clock is for the morning:
It starts at midnight and ends at noon.

This clock is for the afternoon and evening.
It starts at noon and ends at midnight.

© 1998 David C. Cook. Permission granted to reproduce for classroom use only.

Choosing My Actions ✔

Right Things to Do

Is it hard or easy?

Doing my school work on time

Is it . . .

Hard or Easy?

Will you ask for God's help?

YES or No

If you don't use self-discipline,
you'll probably do this instead . . .

Saying kind words instead of being rude

Is it . . .

Hard or Easy?

Will you ask for God's help?

YES or No

If you don't use self-discipline,
you'll probably do this instead . . .

Obeying my parents

Is it . . .

Hard or Easy?

Will you ask for God's help?

YES or No

If you don't use self-discipline,
you'll probably do this instead . . .

Getting ready on time

Is it . . .

Hard or Easy?

Will you ask for God's help?

YES or No

If you don't use self-discipline,
you'll probably do this instead . . .

Watching only the right things on TV

Is it . . .

Hard or Easy?

Will you ask for God's help?

YES or No

If you don't use self-discipline,
you'll probably do this instead . . .

Write something you know you should do

Is it . . .

Hard or Easy?

Will you ask for God's help?

YES or No

If you don't use self-discipline,
you'll probably do this instead . . .

© 1998 David C. Cook. Permission granted to reproduce for classroom use only.

Service Projects

*In addition to the projects listed in these lessons, your class
or church can also serve in the following ways:*

1
Funds, Food, and Fun for others.

Have students save their own money, organize some fund-raisers,
and collect canned food and toys for the church benevolence ministry.

2
Letters of Influence.

Before teaching Lesson 2, get the name and address
of a local politician, the editor of the newspaper, or the head of some other agency
of influence in your community. Have the students write letters to that person,
describing ways they suggest helping and showing respect to those in your
neighborhood and community who need help such as the homeless, the
seriously ill, and those who do not have enough food.

3
Pen Pal Friends.

Ask your pastor or church missions committee for the names
of a missionary family with children and find out when the children's birthdays
are. Help the students establish a pen pal correspondence with the children in
this family. Have the students make a commitment to continue writing letters
to that child or children for at least six months after this unit is over.

4
Cheer Givers.

Divide the class into groups of two to four students each. Have each group plan
weekly visits to someone in your church who lives alone and who would enjoy getting acquainted with students. The planning should include transportation, an
advance call to establish a convenient time, and a discussion of what the students
want to do during the visit. For the first visit they may want to take fresh flowers
and something to read to the person they are visiting. Have the students ask what
they could do for the next three visits and offer such services as writing dictated
letters, reading aloud, simple gardening, and house cleaning assistance.

© 1998 David C. Cook. Permission granted to reproduce for classroom use only.

"I was wrong!"

We're all human. We all mess up. So, why should it be so hard to say, "I was wrong and I'm sorry"? Part of the answer is that our human nature makes admitting sins difficult. We learn to cover up our sins, make excuses, blame others, or simply quit trying. Your students learn these habits, too. By the time they reach the preteen years, these responses are often deeply rooted. If we don't teach them more effective ways of dealing with their sins, these negative responses may reap disastrous consequences.

This unit will give you the opportunity to teach your students how to respond to their sins with honesty and integrity. They will learn to "come clean" by saying six important words: "I was wrong and I'm sorry." In addition, they will learn that no sin can ever keep God from loving them. They will experience God's great patience with them when they struggle with recurring sins. And they will hear over and over about the amazing grace God gives all of us—how He forgives us completely when we confess our sins to Him. All of these things will help students learn to "bounce back" from their sins.

Sin Unit Overview

Unit Verse: If we confess our sins, he is faithful and just and will forgive us. 1 John 1:9.

Unit Affirmation: I CAN BOUNCE BACK FROM MY SINS!

LESSON	TITLE	OBJECTIVE	SCRIPTURE BASE
Lesson #1	I Blew It! . . . Now What?	Students will learn that confessing is the first step to bouncing back from sin.	Gen. 3:1-13, 23; 2 Sam. 11:1-5,14-17; 12:1-7, 13; 1 Sam. 13:5-14; Ex. 2:11-15
Lesson #2	I Feel So Guilty!	Students will learn they can defeat guilty feelings that come from sin by working through four key questions.	Luke 22:31-34; 22:55-62; John 21:15-19
Lesson #3	How Does God Handle My Sin?	Students will discover that no sin can ever make God stop loving them and that God forgives them when they confess their sins.	Rom. 8:1; 5:8; 8:37-39; Ps. 51:6; John 14:26; 16:8; Heb. 10:17
Lesson #4	I Keep Making the Same Sin!	Students will learn three steps to help them overcome recurring sins.	Mark 14:43-52; Acts 13:1-5, 13; 15:36-39; Col. 4:10; 2 Tim. 4:11; Philemon 1:24; Phil. 3:13-14
Also, see page 123 for a list of optional Service Projects that would work well with this unit.			

Partners

Students Bounce Back from Their Sins!

DEAR PARENTS: We hope this newsletter keeps you informed about and involved in what we're doing. After all, you *are your children's most important spiritual leaders. We want to be* your *partner any way we can.*

"I was wrong!"

Sounds simple enough to say, doesn't it? After all, we're all human. We all mess up. But even as adults, admitting our sins is a difficult thing to do.

From the time we are young children we learn to avoid taking responsibility for our wrongs. Instead, we choose instinctively to deal with our sin in unhealthy ways, such as covering it up, making excuses, blaming someone else, or simply giving up. Hopefully, somewhere along the line we have had the opportunity to learn to take responsibility for our sins. Hopefully we've learned to confess our sins to God and receive His forgiveness. It's important for our children to learn that lesson as well.

Over the next four weeks, your children will be learning what it means to "bounce back" from their sin. They will learn to say six important words: "I was wrong and I'm sorry." In addition, they will learn that no sin can ever keep God from loving them. They will experience God's great patience with them when they struggle with recurring sins. And they will hear over and over about the amazing grace God gives all of us—how He forgives us completely when we confess our sins to Him. All of these lessons will help students learn and grow after sinning, instead of making things worse. This process of learning and growing is what we call "bouncing back" from sin.

Unit Verse:
I John 1:9—"*If we confess our sins, he is faithful and just and will forgive us our sins and purify us from all unrighteousness.*"

Unit Affirmation:
I CAN BOUNCE BACK FROM MY SINS!

Principles . . .

PRINCIPLE #1:
Help your children bounce back from sin.

As a parent, it is difficult to watch our children struggle with sin. Our natural instinct is to do everything we can to shield them from sinning. The truth is, however, that no matter how hard we try, we cannot protect our children from their sins. We can, however, serve our children by teaching them how to respond to their sins with honesty and integrity. You can talk to your children about their sins in supportive and loving ways. Your children need to know that no matter what they do, you will continue to love and support them. Once they are assured of that, they will be ready to "bounce back" by taking responsibility for their actions and receiving God's forgiveness.

PRINCIPLE #2:
Guide your children to learn from their sins.

The key word here is *guide*. Lecturing your children about what not to do "next time" rarely accomplishes much. Instead, guide your children through a process. Talk with your children about the following questions:

• **What should I do about it?** Teach your children to do three things after sinning: make things right with God, make things right with others, and make things right with themselves. We make things right with God by confessing our sins and repenting. We make things right with others by apologizing, replacing a broken item, cleaning up a mess we made, etc. We make things right with ourselves by forgiving ourselves as God has forgiven us.

• **What tripped me up?** Help your children examine the true motivation for their wrong actions, such as "I wanted the other kids to like me," or "I lost control of my temper again."

• **What can I learn from this?** Help your children think of an area to work on to avoid making the same wrong action again. Examples: "I need to learn to stand up to my friends"; "I need to learn to ask for help when I don't understand something"; "I need to learn self-control."

PRINCIPLE #3:
Guide your children to take small steps toward overcoming areas of weakness.

Problems such as peer pressure, controlling anger, and lack of self-control take time, practice, and God's help to overcome. Remember that repeating the same wrong action over and over can be discouraging for a child; changing the behavior may seem so overwhelming that the child may simply stop trying. You can encourage your children by reminding them that God can always change our behavior—no matter what it is—if we are willing to depend on Him and if we continue to work at it. Help your children set goals for changes they want to make, and then teach them to identify small, achievable steps they can take to reach their goals. The key here is to help your children identify steps you know they can accomplish. Once they are successful taking a small step, they will feel encouraged to take another step toward their ultimate goal. Example:

• **Unachievable goal:** I will never lose my temper at home again.

• **Achievable goal:** I will go to my room and cool down instead of hitting my brother when I am angry.

pRactiCe

1. Be honest about your own imperfection.
Modeling is always the best teacher! You can teach your children how to take responsibility for their actions by handling your own sin with honesty and integrity. Whenever appropriate, share with your children the lessons you are learning as you work through *your* sins.

2. Make a "Goal Sheet" together.
Help your children set goals to change unwanted behavior by creating a goal sheet. With your children, draw a target on a sheet of paper and write a goal for overcoming an area of weakness in the bull's-eye. For example, if you were making a goal sheet for the problem discussed in the Principles section, you would write: "I will not lose my temper." Then, agree on one small, achievable step your children can take to begin working toward that goal and write it in the first ring. You might write "Ask God to help me" for Step 1. Next, guide your children to think of another small step they can take and write it in the second ring. Be sure the step is concrete and achievable. In this example, you would write, "I will go to my room and cool down instead of hitting my brother when I'm angry." Post the target where it can serve as a reminder to your children. When these steps have been accomplished, sit down with your children again and add another step in the next ring. Continue in this way until your children have achieved the ultimate goal written in the bull's-eye!

3. Memorize 1 John 1:9 and Romans 8:37-39.
Make a game of learning these important verses. One way is to start with the first word of the verse, and then ask someone to say the second word, and so on. When someone misses, start the verse over from the beginning. You can easily play a memory verse game such as this when you're eating dinner or riding in the car. To help with the lengthy Romans 8 passage, encourage your children to make up motions to accompany each phrase. Then give them an opportunity to perform their creation at a family gathering.

Can Bounce Back from My Sins !

"If we confess our sins, he is faithful and just and will forgive us."

1 John 1:9

 Sin

I Blew It! . . . Now What?

Aim: Students will learn that confessing is the first step to bouncing back from sin.

Scripture: Genesis 3:1-13, 23; 2 Samuel 11:1-5, 14-17; 12:1-7, 13; 1 Samuel 13:5-14; Exodus 2:11-15

Unit Verse: If we confess our sins, he is faithful and just and will forgive us. 1 John 1:9

Unit Affirmation: I CAN BOUNCE BACK FROM MY SINS!

1 Setting the Stage (5-10 minutes)

WHAT YOU'LL DO
- Discuss articles about wrong actions that you've cut out of newspapers ahead of time.
- Define sin.

WHAT YOU'LL NEED
- Old newspapers, scissors

PLANNING AHEAD
- Cut out articles from old newspapers about people who have committed some wrong actions.

2 Introducing the Lesson (20 minutes)

WHAT YOU'LL DO
- Discuss four common, unhealthy reactions to sin.
- Write an ending to an unfinished story.

WHAT YOU'LL NEED
- Posterboard or newsprint, copies of the "You Can't Be Serious!" Activity Sheet (page 97), pencils

3 Searching the Scriptures (20 minutes)

WHAT YOU'LL DO
- Create news reports about Bible characters who sinned.

WHAT YOU'LL NEED
- Copies of the "It's A Hot Story" Activity Sheet (page 98)
- Unit Poster

PLANNING AHEAD
- Make the Unit Poster (see directions on page 5 and poster on page 91)

4 Living the Lesson (5-10 minutes)

WHAT YOU'LL DO
- Make an action plan to take responsibility for one past sin.

WHAT YOU'LL NEED
- Copies of the "Bouncing Back" Activity Sheet (page 99)

Lesson 1

✔ Setting the Stage (5-10 minutes)

Ahead of time, find and cut out articles from old newspapers about people who have done something wrong. If you look hard enough, you can find wrong actions in many newspaper stories, for instance: crimes, gang activity, scandals involving public figures, and so on. Spread these articles out on a table.

As students arrive today, have each skim through a number of articles and pick out one that catches his or her attention. After a few minutes, ask students to describe the articles they found.

What's sin? Sin is anything that is wrong in the eyes of God—any wrong action that breaks God's standards.

Some sins make the front page. Some sins don't. Big or small, we all sin. But many people don't how to respond when they sin. In this unit, we're going to find out that our sins don't have to knock us down for the count. We can bounce back.

✔ Introducing the Issue (20 minutes)

Most of the time when we sin, we know it immediately. Almost as soon as we're done with the action, we find ourselves wishing we could take it back. But *knowing* we did something wrong and *saying* the words "I was wrong and I'm sorry" are two different things. We often respond in ways that make everything worse. Some of the most common ways we respond to our sins are: blaming, covering up, making excuses, and giving up.

Distribute copies of the "You Can't Be Serious!" Activity Sheet. Ask for three volunteers to read the roles of Robert, Jeffrey, and Mr. Morales. Discuss: **Both Robert and Jeffrey have done a number of things wrong already. But let's just focus on Jeffrey for now. Did Jeffrey sin? What sins did he commit?** Possible answers: cheated, lied, called Robert names, punched Robert.

We know that Jeffrey should probably say, "I was wrong and I'm sorry." But it doesn't seem like he's ready to do that, does it? Let's talk about some of the responses he might make instead.

Work on the bottom part of the activity sheet together. Brainstorm and write down responses for Jeffrey, at least one per category. For example:
- Blaming: "Why are you calling my dad when it was all Robert's fault?"
- Covering it up: "Please don't tell my dad! I'll do detentions for a week. I'll do anything you want if you just don't tell my dad!"
- Making excuses: "Look, Mr. Morales, I've just had a lot going on at home, lately. You would have blown up, too, if you were in my shoes."
- Giving up: "I keep blowing it! I guess I'll always be this way. I can't change."

Let's think about these responses for a moment. Which of these will help Jeffrey resolve the situation he's in? Which will only make the situation worse? Guide students to see that although all four of these responses are common, they simply aren't helpful. Each response will only make matters worse for Jeffrey by getting him into more trouble or causing him to feel worse.

There is a better way to respond when we sin. We can "come clean." We can simply say, "I was wrong and I'm sorry." Coming clean means confessing you were wrong and accepting the consequences for your actions. When you sin, you have to come clean not just to other people, but to God as well.

Tell students to get back into pairs and ask each pair to write a new ending to the story under the "Right Response" heading at the bottom of the activity sheet. This time the response should illustrate how Jeffrey might come clean and *accept responsibility* for his actions. Have volunteers read their answers out loud. Example: "I admit it. I did copy from Robert's paper, Mr. Morales. I've been going through a lot at home lately. I had to go visit my Mom in the hospital last night, and I came home too tired to study. But I was wrong to cheat, and I'm sorry. Robert, I'm sorry for punching you. I shouldn't have done that."

If Jeffrey responds this way, do you think Mr. Morales will still call his father? Take a few responses. Help students understand that responding with integrity does not keep us from suffering the consequences of our actions. Mr. Morales may still call Jeffrey's dad. Jeffrey may still have a hard time rebuilding his friendship with Robert. But by telling the truth and taking responsibility for his actions, Jeffrey has done the right thing. He has put himself on a path to bounce back and grow from the situation instead of making things worse.

How can Jeffrey "come clean" to God? Help students see that the same basic principle of accepting responsibility for our wrong actions also applies to our relationship with God. Jeffrey should find a time to say to God, "I was wrong and I'm sorry." .

 # Searching the Scriptures (20 minutes)

Covering up, blaming others, making excuses, and running away from sin are not new! Let's look at some people in the Bible who sinned and see how they responded. We'll see which of these people in the Bible bounced back and which people were knocked down for the count. Divide into four groups. Set the stage for this activity by telling students they are all hot shot TV news reporters. Give them their newest assignments by distributing copies of the "It's A Hot Story!" Activity Sheet. Assign each group one of the

Lesson 1

Scripture passages below. They should write their passages at the top of their sheets. First, teams must complete their "investigations" by answering the questions on the sheet. Then each group should plan a brief TV news report to share their findings with the rest of the class. Give the groups guidance as needed. Use the following information as background:

- Genesis 3:1-13—Adam and Eve listened to the serpent, ate the fruit God had forbidden them to eat, and then *blamed* someone else for their sins (Adam blamed Eve and Eve blamed Satan). Although they suffered consequences of their sins (they were expelled from the garden), they went on to fulfill God's plan to populate the earth by having children.
- 2 Samuel 11:1-5, 14-17; 12:1-7, 13—David fell in love with another man's wife and got her pregnant. To *cover up* his sin, David conspired with his military leader to have the woman's husband killed in battle. God then sent Nathan the prophet to David, and Nathan made it clear that what David did was wrong in God's eyes. David then accepted responsibility for his sinful actions and asked for God's forgiveness. David suffered severe consequences for his actions, but he was able to bounce back and continue to serve the Lord. He is still remembered as one of the most faithful kings of Israel.
- 1 Samuel 13:5-14—King Saul's soldiers got frightened and scattered. King Saul was afraid for his life and wanted God's help, so he burned animal sacrifices to God. But God had already told Saul to wait until the prophet Samuel came—so Saul, even though he meant well, disobeyed God. When Samuel finally arrived and confronted Saul, Saul *made excuses* for his sin. We do not have a record that Saul ever accepted responsibility for what he did. As a result, his consequences were clear—he was no longer allowed to remain king.
- Exodus 2:11-15—Moses acted out of rage and killed an Egyptian who was beating up on someone of Moses' Hebrew race. At first, Moses tried to *cover up* his sin by burying the man in the sand. When someone discovered that he had killed the man, Moses ran away. Essentially, Moses *gave up* to avoid taking responsibility for what he did. We do not have a record of Moses ever specifically taking responsibility for that murder. But we do know he continued to worship the Lord and years later obeyed Him by leading the Hebrew people out of slavery.

Say: **We interrupt our nightly news to bring you these breaking stories! We have in our studio today several correspondents who have just returned with incredible stories of famous, well-respected leaders who have committed some serious sins! Here they are for a live report.** Have each group make its report. Conclude by saying: **Even the greatest leaders in the Bible sinned. Then, on top of that, they made their situations worse by blaming others, trying to cover up their sins, making excuses, and giving up!**

Some of them bounced back from their sins and went on to do great things for God. Which ones bounced back? (David and Moses.)

Why do you think they were able to bounce back from their sins? (They eventually came clean—they admitted their sins and took responsibility for their actions. Even though this is not recorded in the Bible in Moses' case, it's implied since he was later used by God.)

Which person was knocked down for the count and never again did something great for God? (Saul.)

What do you think kept Saul from bouncing back from his sin? (Probably because he never came clean with sin.)

Display the Unit Poster and read the Unit Affirmation together: I CAN BOUNCE BACK FROM MY SINS! **We can bounce back when we come clean and say, "I was wrong and I'm sorry."** Read the Unit Verse together: 1 John 1:9—"If we confess our sins, he is faithful and just and will forgive us our sins." Review some definitions that will help students understand this verse.

• CONFESS OUR SINS—Coming clean with God; saying, "I was wrong, God, and I'm sorry."

• FAITHFUL—God keeps His promises. We can trust God to forgive us all the time, every time we confess.

• JUST—God always does the right and fair thing. It's "fair" for God to forgive our sins because Jesus died on the cross for our sins.

✔ Living the Lesson (5-10 minutes)

Distribute pencils and copies of the "Bouncing Back" Activity Sheet. Give students a few minutes to complete the top half of the sheet on their own. Review answers with your students: Situations 1, 5, 7, 8, and 9 are sinful actions. The other actions are not sins. Discuss: **What are some ways we could respond to these sins? Which responses will make things worse? Which responses will help us bounce back?**

Tell students to take a few more minutes and fill out the bottom half of the sheet.

Finally, end with a time of prayer. Encourage each student to silently confess one sin to God and ask for His help to accept responsibility for the sin. Close with a specific prayer for each student.

✔ You Can't Be Serious!

Scene: *During the math test today, Jeffrey started copying answers from Robert's paper. Mrs. Miller saw Robert cover his paper and turn away. She gave Jeffrey an automatic F. During lunch hour, Jeffrey blamed Robert, and the boys got into a fist fight. Mr. Morales, the principal, came out to break it up.*

MR. MORALES:	Okay, you two. Stop it right now! What is this about?
JEFFREY:	He's a loser, that's what!
ROBERT:	I didn't do anything! He just started punching me.
JEFFREY:	You liar! You deserved every punch.
MR. MORALES:	Enough! I can see I'm not going to get any cooperation here. Maybe we should resolve this in my office.
ROBERT:	He was copying from my paper during the math test today, and Mrs. Miller gave him an F.
JEFFREY:	I did not copy from your paper! You're so dumb in math; you're the last person I'd copy from! I got an F just because of you!
ROBERT:	You copied my answers and you know it!
MR. MORALES:	Enough! Robert, I want to see you in my office right now. And you, Jeffrey, I'm placing a call to your father and setting up a time for the three of us to have a conference about this.
JEFFREY:	What? You can't be serious!
MR. MORALES:	And just why wouldn't I be serious?

Jeffrey could say . . .

Negative Responses

Blaming Others:

Covering Up:

Making Excuses:

Giving Up:

The Right Response:

© 1998 David C. Cook. Permission granted to reproduce for classroom use only.

It's a Hot Story! ✔

You are a top news team and have just received a hot tip:
Several key biblical leaders have committed serious sins and not responded very well! Your assignment is to research the details and prepare a report for the evening news. Proceed as follows:

1. Write your Scripture passage here:

   _____ .

2. Discover the facts:

   Who was involved?

   What happened?

   When and where did it happen?

   What was the result?

3. Summary: How did the primary person(s) in this story handle his(their) sin(s) (circle one):

   Blamed someone else   Covered it up   Made excuses   Gave up

4. Then what happened:

   Did this person(s) bounce back? (Circle your answer)

   YES   OR   NO

   If they bounced back, what did he (they) go on to accomplish for God?

5. How could the person(s) in your story have responded the first time?

   He (they) could have . . .

© 1998 David C. Cook. Permission granted to reproduce for classroom use only.

 **Bouncing Back**

Make a check mark next to each action that is sinful.

____ 1. I punched someone when I was angry.

____ 2. I dropped a ball or struck out in baseball.

____ 3. I messed up during a music or dance recital.

____ 4. I missed questions on a test in school.

____ 5. I cheated on a test in school.

____ 6. I forgot to add an ingredient in a recipe.

____ 7. I experimented with illegal drugs.

____ 8. I participated in name calling and teasing someone in my class.

____ 9. I let friends pressure me into doing something I knew was wrong.

____ Other:

Have you ever responded in one of the ways listed below? Make a check mark next to each response you have used when you've sinned in the past.

____ I tried to cover it up so no one would find out I did it.

____ I blamed someone else, even though I knew it was my fault.

____ I made up excuses so it wouldn't look like it was my fault.

____ I tried to run away or hide, hoping it would all just go away.

Now for the hard part! Write down one sinful thing you've done but never accepted responsibility for. Then think of some things you can do to come clean with your sin—to God and to others.

The sinful thing I did is:

What can you say to come clean to God?

What can you do to come clean with others? (For example, do you need to apologize to someone, or return something you took without permission, or pay for something you broke?)

_____

_____

_____

_____

© 1998 David C. Cook. Permission granted to reproduce for classroom use only.

I Feel So Guilty!

Aim: Students will learn they can defeat guilty feelings that come from sin by working through four key questions.

Scripture: Luke 22:31-34; 22:55-62; John 21:15-19

Unit Verse: If we confess our sins, he is faithful and just and will forgive us our sins. 1 John 1:9

Unit Affirmation: I CAN BOUNCE BACK FROM MY SINS!

1 Setting the Stage (5-10 minutes)

WHAT YOU'LL DO
- Create imaginary monsters.

WHAT YOU'LL NEED
- A variety of art supplies and "junk" items, such as empty pop cans, candy bar wrappers, twigs, old newspapers, empty boxes, and discarded costume jewelry

2 Introducing the Issue (20 minutes)

WHAT YOU'LL DO
- Use a visual to illustrate how guilt can become "monstrous."
- Practice using key questions to resolve guilt feelings.

WHAT YOU'LL NEED
- Enlargement of "Guilt Monster" Activity Sheet, index cards, copies of "I Wish I'd Never Done That!" Activity Sheet (page 107), pencils

PLANNING AHEAD
- Make an approximately 3' x 5' enlargement of the "The Guilt Monster" (page 106) by photocopying it onto an overhead transparency, projecting it onto paper which you have taped to the wall, and then tracing the outline with a large marker.

3 Searching the Scriptures (20 minutes)

WHAT YOU'LL DO
- Review the story of Peter's denial of Christ and apply the Guilt Slayer's Questions to Peter's experience.

WHAT YOU'LL NEED
- A long strip of shelf or butcher paper, writing paper, pencils

4 Living the Lesson (5-10 minutes)

WHAT YOU'LL DO
- Participate in a circle of prayer.

WHAT YOU'LL NEED
- Unit Poster

Lesson 2

✔ Setting the Stage (5-10 minutes)

As kids arrive today, direct them to a table where you have laid out a variety of art supplies and other "junk" items they can use to create an imaginary monster. Instruct them to let their imaginations guide them to create a scary or creepy-looking monster of some kind. They can work alone, in pairs, or small groups. When time is up, have students or teams describe their creations to the rest of the class.

Of course, you're not "little kids" anymore. You know that monsters don't really exist. But it can be fun to pretend about monsters sometimes. We like to see them in movies or smash them in video games. Pause to let students talk about monsters they've seen in movies, video games, or elsewhere. **We know monsters are not real, but we face things every day that can seem** *monstrous.* **Some problems we face in our lives make us feel like we're face to face with some beastly, ugly, overwhelming monster. For example, when your parents go through a divorce or you face a huge test. All these things can feel monstrous. What are some other monsters you might face?** Pause for answers. See if anyone mentions "guilt."

Guilt is another monster that attacks us and overwhelms us. Guilt is sometimes the bad feeling we get after we sin. When we sin, we *should* **feel guilty. But, we don't have to feel guilty for long. We're going to find out today how we can defeat the "Guilt Monster!"**

✔ Introducing the Issue (20 minutes)

Ahead of time, photocopy the "Guilt Monster" Activity Sheet onto a transparency. Put the transparency on an overhead projector and project the image onto a large piece of newsprint that you've taped to the wall. The larger the piece of newsprint, the better. Trace the monster onto the newsprint. Take the poster of the Guilt Monster down off the wall, roll it up, and keep it out of sight during the Setting the Stage activity. At this point in the lesson, ask a few volunteers to help you tape it up to the wall.

Place a stack of 3" x 5" index cards on a table. Ask students to think of sins that are common for kids their age to commit. When they think of an example, they should write it on a card and tape it to the poster of the Guilt Monster. Point out how each of the sins listed could cause guilt feelings. Examples of sins: punch someone out of anger, tease or harass classmates just because the other kids are doing it, let peers pressure you into something you know is wrong, tell your parents a lie to cover up something you did.

Lesson 2

It is important to understand that guilt *by itself* is not the monster! Guilt is an important feeling God has given us. Guilt convicts us that we have done something wrong. Any time we sin, we *should* feel guilty. But guilt can sometimes take over and become very troublesome.

How do you know if your guilt feelings have gotten out of control and turned into a Guilt Monster? Guide your students to think of physical and emotional symptoms they experience when they become consumed with guilt feelings. As they think of responses, have them write these on cards and tape them to the Guilt Monster. Examples: stomachaches, headaches, inability to concentrate on school work, loss of appetite, inability to sleep, desire to avoid people we've lied to or hurt in some way, loss of self confidence ("If I messed up once, I might mess up again so I'm afraid to try any more!"). **Symptoms such as these are clear signs that we have not handled our guilt about sin very well. We need to do something to resolve the situation. We can do that by answering a few key questions about our guilt.**

Distribute copies of the "I Wish I Hadn't Done That!" Activity Sheet, assign two volunteers for the roles of Brenda and Mom, and have them read the skit for the class. Following the skit, give students a few minutes to solve the puzzle and fill in the blanks to the "Guilt Slayer's Questions." Here are the answers:

1. **Exactly what did I do wrong?**
2. **What can I do to make it right?**
3. **What tripped me up?**
4. **What can I learn from this?**

Next, have students answer the four questions for Brenda's situation. Use the following as background information to help you facilitate this discussion:

1. Exactly what did Brenda do wrong? Brenda's wrong actions were teasing the new girl in the first place, then continuing to do so after she realized it had gone too far.

When students apply this question to their own guilt feelings, it will help them name exactly what they did. As a result, students will no longer be able to make excuses, blame someone else, or run away from what happened. They can begin to face their guilt with integrity.

2. What can Brenda do to make it right? Brenda can, first of all, confess her sins to God. She can also: apologize to the girl she teased, befriend her, and stand up to her classmates by telling them that she will not continue to do something that hurts another person. Finally, Brenda can forgive herself.

3. What tripped Brenda up? Brenda was tripped up by her fear of looking "weird" in front of her peers.

Sin is not just about behavior. There are always heart issues to look at as well. Answering this question will help students determine what in their hearts kept them from doing what they knew was right. For example, your

Lesson 2

students may do things they know are wrong because they are afraid of losing the approval of their peers, or because they too easily lose their temper.

4. What can Brenda learn from this? Brenda learned that standing up for what she believes is right is more important than going along with what others are doing.

Help your students see that they can learn to strengthen their weak spots and avoid similar sins in the future by answering this crucial question. For example, they may learn that they can avoid such problems by asking for help when they don't understand something in school, or by practicing effective ways of controlling their temper, or by taking a stand for what they know is right.

This is not an easy process to go through. But the reward for struggling with these hard questions is that you can slay the Guilt Monster. You can experience peace and forgiveness.

Display the Unit Poster. Read the Unit Verse together. Say: **The reason we can slay the Guilt Monster is because we are confident that God will forgive us of our sins.** Repeat the Unit Affirmation together: I CAN BOUNCE BACK FROM MY SINS!

☑ Searching the Scriptures (20 minutes)

Dealing with the Guilt Monster is nothing new. The Bible is full of examples of people who struggled with guilt feelings. Let's look at one example from an important person in the Bible—Peter.

Review the story of Peter's denial of Christ by having volunteers read John 13:33-38; Luke 22:55-62; and John 21:15-19. Fill in additional details as needed so that your students understand exactly what happened to Peter and the deep amount of guilt he felt because of his sinful actions. To get students to interact with their reading, have them storyboard the key events in Peter's life. Starting with Peter's declaration of his loyalty to Jesus at the Last Supper and concluding with his interaction with Jesus on the shore following His resurrection, have students break the story down into scenes to draw. When the pictures are complete, display them in the proper order on a long strip of butcher or shelf paper and display it in your room.

> OPTIONAL: If the storyboard turns out well, you might consider having students sign their pictures and then display the completed storyboard in a place where many from your church can enjoy it.

Next, tell your class to put themselves in Peter's shoes at the point when he is weeping over his denial of Christ. Divide into four groups and assign each group one of the four "Guilt Slayer's Questions" (the questions you just reviewed in Introducing the Issue). Pass out pencils and paper and have

students write their assigned question on the top of their paper. Give the groups two or three minutes to discuss how Peter might have answered the questions concerning the sin he committed when he denied that he knew Jesus. Walk around to each group and make sure they're on the right track. Use the following insights as a guide, then have each group report to the rest of the class.

Group 1: *Exactly what did I do wrong?* Peter's sin was to deny three times that He knew Christ.

Group 2: *What can I do to make it right?* First, Peter had to make things right with God. We don't know what Peter prayed when he wept bitterly on the rock, but we can guess that at some point Peter confessed his sin to God and asked for forgiveness. Second, Peter had to make things right with Jesus (In this special situation, Peter had to make amends with Jesus on a human level even after he had already made amends with God on a spiritual level). When you let someone down, the best thing to do is go to that person, apologize, and ask for forgiveness. Finally, Peter had to forgive himself.

Group 3: *What tripped me up?* Perhaps Peter stumbled on his weak spot, his tendency to act without thinking. When asked if he knew Jesus, Peter acted on his first response—to protect himself and his reputation by denying Christ.

Group 4: *What can I learn from this?* Peter learned he needed to rely on God's power to help him in the future. This lesson was very important for Peter to remember, because as he leaned on God's power throughout the rest of his life, he saw God do many powerful and amazing things through him.

✔ Living the Lesson (5-10 minutes)

Gather your students in a circle. **Let's end our class today by talking to God about sins we've committed. We will use the Guilt Slayer Questions to guide our prayer time.**

Ask your students to think of one wrong action they've committed recently that they may still feel guilty about. Then have them bow their heads and close their eyes. Direct their prayer time by reading the following statements, allowing a few moments for silent prayers between each one:

Tell God exactly what you did.

Do you feel sorry toward God? Do you want to stop doing what you know is wrong and do what's right instead? Tell God that.

Were there other people involved? If so, what do you need to do to make it right with them? Do you need to return something or apologize for something? Ask God to show you what you need to do.

If you've confessed your sin and if you've made things right with

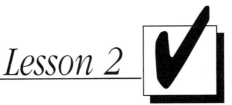

others, you need to know that you are forgiven by God. Thank God for forgiving you.

Now, ask God to show you your weak spot that led to this sin.

Finally, ask God to show you what you can learn from this, and ask Him to help you strengthen your weak spot so you won't repeat this sin in the future.

If time allows, debrief this experience by allowing volunteers the opportunity to share what they prayed about. Encourage students to realize that while it's risky to share in a group setting, each person has something valuable to say and the group may learn from his or her thoughts and insights.

 # The Guilt Monster

© 1998 David C. Cook. Permission granted to reproduce for classroom use only.

 # I Wish I Hadn't Done That!

Scene: *Brenda is sitting on her bed, trying to study, but she can't concentrate. For the past few months, she and her friends have been harassing a Russian girl in her class who was recently adopted by an American family. When the school year started, the girl knew very little English and was frightened of the American school. She insisted on wearing her old clothes because they reminded her of home, and she never made eye contact with any of the kids in the class. The teasing started slowly, but over a period of months Brenda has realized that the teasing has gone way too far. She feels terrible about how she has treated this girl, but she doesn't know what to do about it.*

MOM: Can I come in?

BRENDA: Sure, Mom.

MOM: You look very sad lately, Brenda. What's bothering you?

BRENDA: Nothing, Mom. Honest!

MOM: That's not what your teacher says.

BRENDA: *(Gets tense.)* What do you mean?

MOM: She called today. She's worried about you. Says you aren't participating in class and you're avoiding her. That's not like you, Brenda. You love Mrs. Lee!

BRENDA: *(Looks down and sighs.)* I don't know what to do, Mom. Everything is out of control and I feel so guilty!

MOM: You could start by telling me about it.

BRENDA: Well, it's about this new girl in our class. She just moved here from Russia and some of the kids have been teasing her a lot. I'm not even sure how it all started! We used to laugh when she tried to answer questions—she sounded so funny. Everyone laughed, Mom! It was no big deal! But then some kids started making fun of her all the time and got all the kids in the class to tease her, too.

MOM: And you've been one of the kids teasing this girl?

BRENDA: I didn't mean for it to go this far. I was just doing what the other kids were doing. They would have thought I was weird if I hadn't! But you should have seen her at lunch yesterday. She was all alone, and I think she was crying. I know she needs a friend, and I wanted to talk to her, but I was afraid. All this teasing stuff is out of control, and I should have stopped a long time ago, but I didn't. I wish I'd never done that, Mom!

Guilt Slayer's Questions:

Question #1: __ __ __ __ __ __ __ what did I do __ __ __ __ __?
                    7 26 3 5   22 14 27   25 20 17 16 9

Question #2: __ __ __ __ can I __ __ to __ __ __ __ it __ __ __ __ __?
                25 10 3 22   6 17   15 3 13 7   20 11 9 10 22

Question #3: What __ __ __ __ __ __ __ me __ __?
                       22 20 11 18 18 7 6   23 18

Question #4: What can I __ __ __ __ __ from __ __ __ __?
                          14 7 3 20 16   22 10 11 21

CODE: Figure out the letters to place in the blanks by subtracting 2 from the number and then finding the letter of the alphabet that corresponds to that number. Example: 5-2=3; the third letter of the alphabet is C. Therefore, 5 = C.

© 1998 David C. Cook. Permission granted to reproduce for classroom use only.

Sin

How Does God Handle My Sin?

Aim: Students will discover that no sin can ever make God stop loving them and that God will forgive them when they confess their sins.

Scripture: Romans 8:1; Romans 5:8; Romans 8:37-39; 1 John 1:9; Psalm 51:6; John 14:26; John 16:8; Hebrews 10:17

Unit Verse: If we confess our sins, he is faithful and just and will forgive us our sins. 1 John 1:9

Unit Affirmation: I CAN BOUNCE BACK FROM MY SINS!

1 Setting the Stage (5-10 minutes)

WHAT YOU'LL DO

• Create a "living collage" of a perfect family.

2 Introducing the Lesson (20 minutes)

WHAT YOU'LL DO

• Design the ideal family.

WHAT YOU'LL NEED

• Copies of the "Create-A-Family" Activity Sheet (page 113), pencils

3 Searching the Scriptures (20 minutes)

WHAT YOU'LL DO

• Learn how God responds when we make mistakes.

WHAT YOU'LL NEED

• "What Does God Think?" visual aid, Scripture (see Scripture listed above) written on 3" x 5" cards, Unit Poster

PLANNING AHEAD

• Prepare the "What Does God Think?" visual aid by writing the title across the top of a posterboard and then dividing it into three columns. Label the columns: "God's Response to Sin"; "My Response to God"; and "God's Final Response."

4 Living the Lesson (5-10 minutes)

WHAT YOU'LL DO

• Give an opportunity for kids to become part of God's family and experience God's forgiveness.

WHAT YOU'LL NEED

• Copies of the "Honest to God" Activity Sheet (page 114)

Lesson 3

✔ Setting the Stage (5-10 minutes)

As students enter, begin to talk to them about what an "ideal" family would look like. Discuss questions like: **What kinds of things would the family do? How would family members relate to each other?** Divide into two groups and tell each group to make a "living collage" that represents an ideal family. In a living collage, students depict a scene by staying in the same pose without talking. For example, two students might choose to pose as a father and son playing catch together. Posed students can show some motion, but it has to be the same movement repeated over and over again, like a father making a throwing motion. It would be best if all motions were made slowly. As some students arrive late, explain what's happening in the collages, then ask them to choose to join one of the two collages and depict a new activity.

When all students have arrived and the collages are complete, compliment students on their creativity, then have them sit down. Discuss: **How are these collages of "ideal families" different than families in the real world?**

✔ Introducing the Issue (20 minutes)

If you had the opportunity to improve your family, what would you change? Today you have the opportunity to design a family the way you would like it to be! Pass out copies of the "Create-A-Family" Activity Sheet and have students complete it in groups of three or four. After a few minutes, come back to discuss and debrief all the groups' answers. Be aware that there are at least two places where it will be important for you to add insight.

When you debrief Question 3 ("What rules should the family have?"), ask tough questions as needed that will help students see that a loving family has appropriate rules and boundaries. For example, if students want to make a rule that "Kids can eat anything they want," discuss what would happen if kids were allowed to eat just junk food all the time—they would certainly get sick! If students want to make a rule like "Kids can watch as much TV as they want," discuss some of the possible consequences—they might develop lazy minds, etc.

When you discuss Question 7 ("What happens when a child does something wrong?"), help students understand that loving parents discipline their children. But nothing a child does—no matter how wrong—could ever change most parents' love for their child! Ask students to talk about how discipline happens in their families. If you are a parent, this is an excellent opportunity to share how you love your children no matter what they do. If you are not a parent, you may be able to share about a relationship in which you have experienced unconditional love.

> OPTIONAL: Divide into groups of three or four and ask each group to create a portrait of the ideal family you discussed, using newsprint and markers. Have each group share its poster with the rest of the class and post it on the wall.

Today we are going to talk about what happens when we do something wrong in another family—God's family. Does God stop loving us when we do something wrong? NO! God loves us more perfectly than *any* **earthly parent could possibly love us! There is absolutely nothing you can do that will ever make a good parent love you any more or less. The same is true of God. He loves you right now this second more than you can know—and nothing you ever do can change that! But, like a good parent, God doesn't just overlook our sins. He responds to them in the best way possible.**

✔ Searching the Scriptures (20 minutes)

Ahead of time, prepare the "What Does God Think?" visual aid by writing the title across the top of a piece posterboard, then dividing it into three columns. Label the columns: "God's Response to Sin"; "My Response to God"; and "God's Final Response."

Also, use the following "Bible drill" to get students ready to read selected Scripture: Ask students to lay their Bibles in front of them and place their hands at their sides. Read the references from your reference cards one at a time and have students race to look them up. Give the cards containing the references to those who find them first, and have those students place the references in their Bibles as bookmarks so they can find and read the verses later.

> OPTIONAL: If you have unchurched students in your group that might be intimidated by a Bible drill, you may want to choose a few students ahead of time and give each one a Scripture reference to look up.

What is God's response when we sin? What if you cheated on a test at school . . . how will God respond? Let students share their ideas. Then discuss the information below. First, ask the numbered question out loud and take a few responses. Then have the students who have the reference cards for the Scripture listed after that question read their verses. Finally, use the commentary that follows each question to help facilitate a discussion so the Bible's answer to the numbered question becomes more clear. When the questions are answered, tape the reference cards to the appropriate column on the "What Does God Think?" visual aid.

God's Response to Sin: Love *and* Discipline.

1. Will God stop loving us?

Read: Romans 8:1; 5:8; 8:37-39.

No! He loved us so much He sent Jesus to take our punishment. If we believe in Jesus, we can trust in God's unfailing love for His children. Help

your kids see that God's acceptance of them is based on Jesus' death on the cross and therefore it is never tied to their actions—good or bad.

2. Like a good parent, God will discipline the things we do wrong. How might He do that?

Read: Hebrews 12:5-11.

When we become God's children through faith in Jesus, God deals with disobedient children similar to how the best human parents discipline their children. It becomes necessary to discipline disobedience, yet God is loving and He always wants the very best for us.

Our Response to God: Confession

3. What should our response be when it becomes clear that we have sinned?

Read: 1 John 1:9 and Psalm 51:6.

All God asks of us is that we confess—we must come clean and tell the truth about our sins. Help students see that we confess our sins in response to both God's unconditional love and His discipline. If God just loved us but didn't discipline us, it would be easy for us to continue sinning. It might seem to us that it didn't matter to God whether we sinned or not. But if God just disciplined us and didn't love us, we might not want to confess our sins to God. We might be afraid of God's condemnation of us.

God's Response to Our Confession: Forgiveness

4. What is God's response when we tell Him the truth about our sins?

Read: 1 John 1:9 again, and Hebrews 10:17.

God freely forgives our sins when we confess to Him. But He does much more than that; He forgets that they ever happened in the first place! God does not keep a giant scoreboard of our sins. When we confess them honestly, He removes them forever!

Display the Unit Poster and read the Unit Affirmation together: I CAN BOUNCE BACK FROM MY SINS! **We can be honest with God and He will not condemn us. He forgives us completely.** Read the Unit Verse one more time.

✔ Living the Lesson (5-10 minutes)

Having God as our Father is a very special privilege that is possible only because He sent His Son, Jesus, to die on the cross to take our punishment. But being part of God's family is not an automatic thing. The Bible says clearly that we must first of all believe in Jesus as our Savior in order to receive eternal life.

Distribute copies of the "Honest to God" Activity Sheet and read through it together. Encourage students to sign their cards as a commitment of their hearts and lives to God. Be sure they understand that if they have already given their hearts to Jesus, they need not do so again, but they can sign the card as a way of thanking God for the privilege of being in His family. Students who have already made a commitment of their hearts and lives to Christ should use the bottom half of the resource as well. This part of the resource allows students to get honest with God about their struggles.

In closing, ask your students to thank God for His gift of forgiveness. Remind them that nothing can ever separate them from God's love for them. Invite students who have never done so to open their hearts to God for the first time and ask Him to make them a member of His family. If they believe on the Lord Jesus, He has promised to save them. Invite any students who make this commitment to tell you about it after class.

 # Create-a-Family

Directions: *If you could create the perfect family—one that met everyone's needs and helped the kids grow up in a healthy way—what would it be like? Work with the others in your group to create a picture of that kind of a family.*

1. Who are the members of your family? *Include as many as you want, including grandparents and other relatives.*

2. What things does this family do together?

3. What are the rules in this family?

4. How do the family members treat each other?

5. What jobs or chores does each family member do?

6. What is the best, or most important, part about living in this family?

7. What happens when a child does something wrong? How do the parents respond?

© 1998 David C. Cook. Permission granted to reproduce for classroom use only.

Honest to God!

1 John 1:9 — If we confess our sins, he is faithful and just and will forgive us our sins and purify us from all unrighteousness.

Dear God,

Thank You that You loved me so much You sent Jesus to take the punishment for my sins. I ask You to forgive me for all the sins I have committed and I give my heart to You so You can make me a member of Your family! I am believing Christ for eternal life. Thank You that I am becoming part of Your family. I want to live for You, so I ask for Your help when temptations to sin come to me.

Love,

Dear God,

I know that I can be honest with You about my struggles and my sins.

I need to tell You that one area I am currently having trouble in is . . .

I confess my sins to You. In my own words that means . . .

Thank You for accepting me for who I am and helping me grow into all I can be. In my own words that means . . .

Love,

© 1998 David C. Cook. Permission granted to reproduce for classroom use only.

Notes

 **Mistakes**

I Keep Making the Same Sin!

Aim: Students will learn three steps to help them overcome recurring sins.

Scripture: Mark 14:43-52; Acts 13:1-5, 13; 15:36-39; Colossians 4:10; 2 Timothy 4:11; Philemon 1:24; Philippians 3:13-14

Unit Verse: If we confess our sins, he is faithful and just and will forgive us our sins. 1 John 1:9

Unit Affirmation: I CAN BOUNCE BACK FROM MY SINS!

1 Setting the Stage (5-10 minutes)

WHAT YOU'LL DO
*   Learn how to sign a song.

WHAT YOU'LL NEED
*   A person to teach kids how to sign a song, or a sign language book

2 Introducing the Lesson (20 minutes)

WHAT YOU'LL DO
*   Discover three steps to overcoming sin.

WHAT YOU'LL NEED
*   Copies of the "I Did It Again!" Activity Sheet (page 121)
*   OPTIONAL: board game for a prop

3 Searching the Scriptures (20 minutes)

WHAT YOU'LL DO
*   Study how John Mark changed over a period of time.
*   Create an Encouragement Poster.

WHAT YOU'LL NEED
*   Posterboard, markers

PLANNING AHEAD
*   Make an example of an Encouragement Poster ahead of time (see Searching the Scriptures).

4 Living the Lesson (5-10 minutes)

WHAT YOU'LL DO
*   Sign a contract to work on one area of weakness.

WHAT YOU'LL NEED
*   Unit Poster, copies of "Reach for the Goal!" Activity Sheet (page 122), pencils

Lesson 4

✔ Setting the Stage (5-10 minutes)

Invite a guest to your class who knows sign language and can teach your class how to sign a favorite praise song. (Or look up the signs up in a book and teach them to your class.) Keep working on the signs until students master it and gain a sense of accomplishment.

We just worked together as a class to accomplish a goal. Along the way, we made some mistakes, didn't we? Most of us did not sign the song perfectly the first time. But at the end, we were able to sing and sign our song very well! What made the difference? (Practicing; learning from our mistakes.)

We can apply this same principle to almost anything—if we keep practicing and learning, we can do almost anything! This same principle can even help us overcome sin to become the people God wants us to be.

✔ Introducing the Issue (20 minutes)

Invite two of your class members to perform the skit, "I Did It Again!" Pass out copies of the activity sheet and let the two volunteers read the skit for the class. Play the part of Mom yourself (or change the role to "Dad" if you're male.) Introduce the skit by saying: **Is there any sin in your life that you find yourself making over and over again? Recurring sins can discourage us and even take away our self-confidence. Maybe more importantly, they keep us from becoming the kind of people God wants us to be. Here's a story about one kid who struggled with a recurring sin.**

After the skit, discuss: **What sin did Robby keep making over and over?** (He did wrong and hurtful things when he got angry.) **Do you think he meant it when he said, "I want to stop, Mom. Honest!"** (Probably. It seems like Robby was *trying* to change his behavior but having a difficult time doing so.) **Do you think Robby may be right when he said, "Maybe I just can't change!"** (No! God can change our behavior if we are willing to depend on Him and if we continue to work at it.) **What are some other sins that can be recurring, like sinful "habits" we want to quit but make anyway, over and over?** (Using bad language, using drugs or alcohol, teasing and hurting a classmate, acting in wrong ways when we get angry, etc.). **How do we feel when we end up repeating the same sinful habit over and over again?** (Discouraged; like a failure; like we want to quit trying.)

Rather than give up, like Robby wanted to do in the skit, you can overcome sin you struggle with by following a few important steps.

Write the following on the board:

Step 1. Be honest!

Step 2. Ask for help when you need it.

Step 3. Take small steps toward change.

Lesson 4

Have students repeat Step 1 out loud: "Be honest!" Tell them to repeat it again with enthusiasm. Discuss: **Was Robby being honest about his struggle?** (Yes, he and his mom had obviously been discussing it for some time.) **Robby was honest with himself and with his mom. Who are some other people we can be honest with about our struggles?** (We need to admit our struggles out loud to people we trust and most importantly, confess our struggles to God.)

Have students read Step 2 out loud: "Ask for help when you need it." Tell them to repeat it again with enthusiasm. **How could Robby ask for help with his problem?** He could start by praying to God to help him remember to stop before he responds in anger. He could also ask his mom or other family members to help him set goals (see Step 3). **Who are some people we can ask to help us overcome our sin?** (God, parents, trusted adults like teachers, coaches, counselors, and church leaders, as well as Christian friends.)

Have students read Step 3 out loud: "Take small steps towards change." Hopefully this time they jumped right in with enthusiasm on the first try. Draw a target (three or four concentric circles) on the chalkboard. **What change does Robby want to make? What is his goal or his "bull's-eye'?** Take responses, then write something like "No more hurtful actions when I'm angry" in the bull's-eye. Say: **Overcoming recurring sins is hardly ever accomplished in one giant leap. Success often comes slowly. We must learn to set** *achievable* **goals. Achievable goals are small steps we can take successfully.** Have students brainstorm some small steps Robby can take to accomplish his ultimate goal, writing one step on each of the rings of the target. Start with something manageable, such as "apologize when I act in hurtful ways." **This is a goal Robby could manage, and when Robby does apologize, it will help him feel like he has done something positive, rather than just feeling likes he's blown it one more time.** Write this inside the largest concentric circle. Once Robby is successful taking his first step, he can start working on taking other steps, such as "Walk away without throwing things or hitting my brother." Write that step on the next ring. **Each small step Robby can manage will help him feel successful and encourage him to keep moving closer to his ultimate goal.**

Searching the Scriptures (20 minutes)

Overcoming sin is never easy. But with time, practice, and, most of all, God's help, we can do it! Let's take a look at one person, John Mark, who struggled to overcome some sinful things in his life.

Read Mark 14:43-52. Tradition tells us that John Mark was the author of this Gospel, that he was a good friend of Peter (1 Peter 5:13), and that Peter

Lesson 4

helped him write the Gospel. Therefore, it is very possible that the young man referred to in verse 52 is actually Mark himself, since it was not uncommon for writers in that day to use the third person when referring to themselves. It is likely that as a young man Mark knew about Jesus and on occasion followed Him. He may even have become acquainted with Peter in this way. However, on the night of Jesus' arrest, John Mark was terrified and ran away from the soldiers rather than standing up for Jesus.

Read Acts 13:1-5, 13. Next, we discover that when the church in Antioch sent Barnabas and Paul off on their first missionary trip, Mark went with them as a helper. Now we need to use our imagination. Do you suppose that young Mark wanted very much to go with his heroes? Perhaps he even begged to go along! It may be that the church leaders were glad to send him as a way to help him grow; or, it may be that some of them argued that he was too young and should wait at home a few more years. At any rate, everyone finally agreed to send him along. However, he did not make it for very long! In Pamphylia, John Mark left Paul and Barnabas and returned home.

Read Acts 15:36-39. Here we learn more about Mark's departure from the first missionary journey. Paul argued vehemently against taking John Mark along again and thought that by leaving, John Mark had proven himself unreliable. Paul felt so strongly about this that he was not even willing to give him a second chance! But later, John Mark was willing to try again. Perhaps, by this point in the story, Mark felt badly about his first failure and had worked hard to prepare himself for another opportunity. Do you think he felt scared that he would make another mistake by going on this trip when he couldn't make it through the first one? But John Mark's heart was sincere, and he wanted very much to share his faith in Christ by going on this trip. Thankfully, Barnabas stood up for Mark and was willing to separate from his missionary partner Paul to make sure Mark got another chance.

Read Colossians 4:10; 2 Timothy 4:11; Philemon 1:24. We don't have any more accounts of John Mark's adventures, except for these references. What they tell us, however, is that he finally reached his goal and stood up for Jesus and told others about Him. In these verses, Mark is greeted as a brother and fellow minister of the gospel. Even Paul came to respect him! Our conclusion? In spite of Mark's rocky beginning, he kept at it. With God's help and with the help of others who believed in him, he overcame his fear and accomplished his ultimate goal.

What kept recurring in John Mark's life? (He had a habit of quitting, or giving up.)

How did it keep him from growing into the person God wanted Him to be? (One example: God apparently had plans to use John Mark on the first missionary journey, but Mark turned back instead.)

How might you guess John Mark was finally able to conquer his recurring sin? (We can guess that he was honest about his sin, asked for help, and set achievable goals.)

Like John Mark, we can overcome sins that we commit repeatedly. The starting point is trusting God to help us. In fact, God's great power is the most important weapon we have to reach our ultimate goals!

Pass out paper and markers and make a poster or posters to celebrate the power God can give us over recurring sins. For best results, make your own "Encouragement Poster" ahead of time to give students a model. For example, you might draw a poster that showed a picture of you being held in God's hands with the slogan "I can do it . . . God can help!"

☑ Living the Lesson (5-10 minutes)

Display the Unit Poster and have students repeat the Unit Affirmation together: "I CAN BOUNCE BACK FROM MY SINS!" **This affirmation is true, even when you struggle with committing the same sin over and over again.**

Now distribute copies of the "Reach for the Goal!" Activity Sheet and read Philippians 3:13-14, which is printed on the top of the sheet. **Paul is saying here that he hasn't got his ultimate goal yet (to be totally clean of any sin), but he keeps "pressing on," or trying as hard as he can to get there. We can take that same attitude toward our sins.**

Direct students to think of one sin that recurs often in their life. Since there's not enough room in the bull's-eye, have students write down an "ultimate goal" at the top of the page. Encourage students to write, "Ask for God's help" in the first, largest ring. Next, guide students to think of one small step they can take toward accomplishing their ultimate goal and have them write that step in the second ring. Work with the students to help them identify a step that is concrete and achievable. They can fill in the remaining circles with more difficult goals as they continue to work through the sheet on their own (once they meet one goal, they can set another, and so on).

End this lesson with a time of prayer. Allow students an opportunity to pray aloud for God's power to take the steps they just identified. Then close with a specific prayer for each of your students. If you know your students' goals, pray specifically for them; ask God to give them the power to be successful.

 # I Did It Again!

Characters: *Robby; his younger brother, Sean; and their Mom.*
Scene: *Robby and Sean are playing Monopoly.*

SEAN: Okay! I need a nine to land on Boardwalk! *(He rolls the dice.)* All right! I made it! I'm gonna buy Boardwalk to go with Park Place! *(He waves the Park Place card at Robby and moves his piece to Boardwalk.)*

ROBBY: No way, Sean! You cheated! You needed ten spaces and you only got nine! Move it back!

SEAN: *(Looks surprised.)* I did not! I needed nine and I got it! I'm buying Boardwalk! Here's the money; now hand it over!

ROBBY: I'm not playing with cheaters! *(Crosses his arms over his chest.)*

SEAN: Fine! I'll just get it myself. *(Reaches for the card.)*

ROBBY: *(Angry)* No you're not! *(Knocks all the pieces and cards on the floor and pushes Sean off his chair as he storms off stage.)*

SEAN: Hey, quit it!

MOM: *(Enters.)* Sean, what's going on in here? *(Looks at the game and Sean sitting on the floor and sighs).* Never mind; I think I can figure it out! Go find your brother and send him to me.

SEAN: OK, Mom. *(Exits.)*

ROBBY: *(Enters, hanging his head.)* I did it again, huh Mom?

MOM: Robby, you promised me you wouldn't act this way any more. You should never throw things and push people around when you're angry.

ROBBY: I want to stop, Mom. Honest! But when I'm really mad, I just keep doing the same stuff over and over. Maybe I just can't change!

© 1998 David C. Cook. Permission granted to reproduce for classroom use only.

Reach for the Goal!

MY ULTIMATE GOAL!: _____

Philippians 3:13-14—

… But one thing I do: Forgetting what is behind and straining toward what is ahead, I press on toward the goal …

STEP ONE: Ask God's power to change!

STEP TWO:

STEP THREE:

STEP FOUR:

My Goal

© 1998 David C. Cook. Permission granted to reproduce for classroom use only.

Service Ideas

Work with children of prisoners.

This project will sensitize your students to the fact that sometimes kids must suffer because of the sins of their parents. Ask your pastor or the person at your church responsible for community outreach for the names of organizations in your area that work with prisoners and their families. Perhaps the most notable is Project Angel Tree, which provides gifts for prisoners' families at Christmas.

Ask a representative to come to speak to your group about the effects that sins committed by those now in prison have had on their families. A local representative can also suggest projects for your class, such as writing to a child whose parent is in prison, delivering food baskets to needy families, or hosting a party for children of prisoners.

Walk for your local crisis pregnancy center.

Invite a representative to address your kids concerning the difficulties facing young girls who get pregnant without being married. The representative can also tell how the center helps the girls. Your class can help with this work by participating in the center's annual fund-raising event, which for many crisis centers may be a walk-a-thon. If the center in your area does not have an organized, annual fund-raiser, involve your class in a fund- raiser of your own, such as a car wash or bake sale, and donate the funds to the center.

Participate in a drug awareness program.

Find out about the programs in your community designed to educate kids about drugs and alcohol and work with one of them to plan a special day for your class. You can hold a rally at your church or plan a field trip to a local adolescent substance abuse treatment center. Whichever you choose, be sure to include an opportunity for students to share what they have learned with others in your church. They could prepare a large banner with an anti-drug message and hang it in a prominent place in your building, or they could write and perform a puppet show for one of the younger Sunday school classes.

© 1998 David C. Cook. Permission granted to reproduce for classroom use only.